BUSINESS AND ECONOMIC DEVELOPMENT IN SAUDI ARABIA

Also by J. W. Wright, Jr

SAUDI ARABIA: Tradition and Transition (*co-editor with Abdulaziz Al-Sweel*)

Business and Economic Development in Saudi Arabia

Essays with Saudi Scholars

Edited by

J. W. Wright, Jr
Assistant Professor of Business Management
Washington College
Chestertown, MD

in cooperation with the Saudi Arabian Cultural Mission to the United States, Washington, DC

First published 1996 by
MACMILLAN PRESS LTD
Houndmills, Basingstoke, Hampshire RG21 6XS
and London
Companies and representatives
throughout the world

ISBN 0–333–62531–5 hardcover
ISBN 0–333–67428–6 paperback

A catalogue record for this book is available
from the British Library.

10 9 8 7 6 5 4 3 2 1
05 04 03 02 01 00 99 98 97 96

Printed in Great Britain by
The Ipswich Book Company Ltd
Ipswich, Suffolk

The Cultural Mission dedicates this collection to

His Royal Highness Prince

Bandar bin Sultan
for his service as Saudi Arabia's
Ambassador to the United States

the editor likewise makes a dedication to

Davy H. McCall,
John R. Presley and
Rodney E. Wilson

for their many contributions to the
field of Middle Eastern economics

Contents

List of Tables

Prologue

From its inception *Business and Economic Development in Saudi Arabia* was intended to introduce business men and women, faculty members and students of business and economics, government officials and lay readers interested in the Kingdom to the complexities of the cultural, economic and legal issues that determine business practices in Saudi Arabia. Although it should prove very influential in the Middle Eastern studies community, we anticipate that its major audience will be in the related areas of business, development, economics and international studies. The scope and variety of the studies in the volume make it suitable as a textbook for courses in Arab studies, comparative and international economics, industrial planning, socioeconomic studies and government planning.

The evidence presented in each of the articles, historical and contemporary, will make the collection valuable for anyone interested in understanding business in the Kingdom of Saudi Arabia. We would like to emphasise, however, that the broad accessibility of the text is in no way derived from a relaxation of scholarly rigour, but rather results from the approach taken by the contributors. This practical orientation is greatly needed in studies about business and the economy in Saudi Arabia. Moreover we feel there needs to be increased recognition that Saudi Arabia is no longer only an oil economy, but rather that it boasts a diversified commercial environment. We feel also the increased attention Saudi Arabia and its neighbours have received since the Gulf War is manifest in renewed business relationships between US contractors and companies indigenous to the Kingdom. This approach, which combines historical perspective, academic research and practical observations, makes the book timely reading for executives wishing to do business in the Kingdom.

DR HAMAD AL-SALLOOM
Cultural Attaché for the
Saudi Arabian Cultural
Mission to the United States

Acknowledgements

Many people have helped in the creation of this collection of articles. First among these are the people who worked at the Saudi Arabian Cultural Mission in the USA, including Drs Hamad Al-Saloom, Abdulaziz Al-Sweel, Abdul Mohsin Hellal and Mohammad Mattar, and Afaf Marsot, Wahid El-Demerdash, Barbara Bryant and Richard Bianci among others.

Many people at Washington College have been instrumental in bringing this project to publication. The two people who deserve the most thanks are Dawn Baker and Andrew Evans, who worked for many hours on the manuscript. W. Timothy Kirk has provided necessary computer support for the project, and Lida Daves Baldwin, Geraldine Fisher, Victoria Sawyer, Jean Simonian, Jefford Vahlbusch and Beverly Wolf deserve thanks for serving as reviewers of the articles submitted by the authors. Marc Brewen, Michael Hanifee, Tony Higgins, Jennifer Hozik, Kristin Kjowski, Jennifer Sands and Chris Vaughn helped to verify the citations used in the project. President Charles H. Trout, Provost Gene Wubbles, other Deans of the College and the members of Academic Council provided much-needed funding for the research for this project. In addition, Suzanne Stetkevych, Alan Douglas and Fedwa Malti-Douglas have all been exceptional mentors throughout the project, as have J. Wayne and M. Diane Wright. Laura Nicely, Harold and Hazel Midkiff, and Jim and Alice Wright deserve credit for being supportive of my work over the years.

We wish to thank our friends at Macmillan who have worked with us on this volume. Giovanna Davitti and Timo Farmiloe have been very helpful and patient with this project. Their comments and suggestions have made the text better in many ways. Keith Povey and his staff also provided valuable help with the manuscript and its index. John R. Presley served as a reviewer of the book, and his comments allowed us to produce a much more substantive manuscript for publication. As always, he has been very supportive, which is greatly appreciated. Rodney Wilson offered many constructive comments on my thesis when it was given as a lecture at the University of Durham.

Finally, we wish to thank the officials at the Saudi Arabian Ministry of Information for reading, improving and approving the text for publication. Their work is greatly appreciated.

J. W. WRIGHT, JR

Notes on the Contributors

A. M. M. Abdul-Rahman is a professor at King Saud University in Riyadh. Dr Abdel-Rahman specialises in the study of industry and corporate structures within the Kingdom. He has published articles with econometric models on Saudi business development, and he has produced research on the micro-economic effects of government policies. Dr Abdul-Rahman is a well-known consultant for Saudi firms and for American companies operating in the Kingdom.

Abdulrahman Al-Aali is one of the Kingdom's foremost consultants on exporting. An advisor to the Saudi Export Development Center, Dr Al-Aali has also conducted feasibility studies and led executive training seminars in various Gulf Arab countries and in the USA. He is Chair of the Business Administration Department at King Saud University. In 1993–4 he was a Fulbright Fellow at George Washington University in Washington, DC.

Abdullah H. Albatel is an Assistant Professor in the Department of Economics at King Saud University in Riyadh, Saudi Arabia, where his specialty is the Kingdom's financial institutions. His dissertation, 'The Roles of Financial institutions in Economic Development: Savings, Investment and Income Growth – The Case of Saudi Arabia', is being revised for publication in book form.

Bandar al-Hajjar is Assistant Professor in the Department of Economics at King Faisal University in Dhahran, Saudi Arabia. Specialising in socioeconomic factors that affect development, Al-Hajjar has worked closely in the Eastern Province's small business community to develop models for increased productivity in the Kingdom's manufacturing sector. He and John Presley have published several articles and lectures on this topic.

Hamad Al-Salloom. As Cultural Attaché for the Saudi Arabian Cultural Mission to the United States, Dr Hamad Al-Salloom has supported both intellectually and financially work on various publication projects on the Kingdom. The most recent of these have been *Saudi Arabia: A Kingdom in Transition*, and *Saudi Arabia: Tradition and Transition*, which were printed by the Mission. He also supported this project and wrote the Preface.

Salah Al-Suhaibani is a professor at the College of Agricultural Engineering at King Saud University in Riyadh, Saudi Arabia. Dr Al-Suhaibani has been active in the planning process for agricultural development and is considered a specialist in the field. His writings on the Kingdom's agricultural policies appear in various Arabic publications. His works on comparative economics have been printed in Saudi Arabia and the United States.

Salayman H. Atieh is an Associate Professor of Accounting and Managerial Information Systems at the College of Industrial Management at King Fahd University of Petroleum and Minerals, Dhahran, Saudi Arabia. In recent years Dr Atieh has specialised in the development of industries funded by the Saudi Basic Industries Corporation. In 1991 he published an article about the comptroller's specific roles in SABIC-sponsored companies.

Muhktar M. Ballool is Chair Emeritus of the Department of Business at King Saud University, Riyadh. He is the author of a number of articles on the Saudi Arabian economy, ranging in topic from econometric modelling to development planning to management training. He has written several books and papers in Arabic and English about the Kingdom's economy. Dr Ballool is a foremost private sector consultant on business development.

Abdulrahman Garawi. As Deputy Director of the Saudi Arabian Agricultural Bank and supervisor of the Bank's management training programmes, Abdulrahman Garawi has become one of the Kingdom's leading experts on human resource development. He specialises in the training of managers in the agricultural and agricultural finance sectors. He is also a leading consultant on agribusiness and agri-industry development in the Kingdom.

Hani Khashoggi, an Associate Professor at King Saud University, has specialised in recent years on the migration and repatriation of labour in the Middle East in general and in Saudi Arabia in particular. Much of Dr Khashoggi's research and writing in this area has also involved analysis of the Kingdom's training environments and how labour importation has affected the managerial abilities and opportunities of Saudi firms.

M. M. Metwally has held a variety of posts at international universities, most recently that of research professor at Kuwait University. Dr Metwally has also taught or pursued research in universities in Australia, the UK and the United States. His major interest is the study of how business organisations and structures affect managerial and production performance. He is a Professor of Economics at King Saud University, Riyadh.

Faisal A. Mubarak is Chair of the Department of Urban Planning at King Saud University, Riyadh. Dr Mubarak is one of the leading scholars on the evolution of Saudi Arabia's built environment, having offered the field many models and articles on improving the flow of development planning in the Kingdom. He is an administrative, planning and training consultant to a variety of ministries and companies operating in the Kingdom.

John R. Presley is Chair of the Department of Economics and Director of the Banking Centre at Loughborough University in the United Kingdom. He has built his career around the study of the Saudi Arabian economy. He has written one edition of *A Guide to the Saudi Arabian Economy* and co-authored a second edition, edited a collection on Islamic banking and published widely in US, Arab and UK academic journals.

Mary E. Schmidt. A consultant to the Popular Participation Learning Group at the World Bank in Washington, DC, Mary Schmidt has proven abilities in development planning in Middle Eastern countries, and she has pursued a consulting research career in development at the World Bank. Her current publications revolve around issues affecting the use of social funds and participatory development in Arab and other countries.

Christopher M. Vaughn wrote his contribution to this book after completing research at the Arab Institute for Bank Studies at the University of Jordan. He has presented a number of lectures on labour relations between the Kingdoms of Jordan and Saudi Arabia at prominent venues, including the 1993 British Society for Middle Eastern Studies conference. He is currently a management development specialist with the Peace Corps.

J. W. Wright, Jr is an Assistant Professor of Business Management at Washington College, where he specialises in Middle East trade relations. A Malone Fellow in Arab and Islamic Studies, he has lectured on the Kingdom at the Universities of Cambridge, Chicago, Durham, Indiana, Princeton, St. Andrews, and Yale, as well as at the Smithsonian Institution and World Bank conferences. He is co-editor of *Saudi Arabia: Tradition and Transition.*

Introduction

The discovery of oil in the 1920s in the Kingdom of Saudi Arabia resulted in a race towards modernisation that was more rapid than any seen outside the Arabian Gulf region. Few economies have witnessed such accelerated economic growth as that caused by infrastructure construction and chattel procurement during the second and third Saudi Five Year Development Plans. As a result the Kingdom's ports and airports are now among the largest in the world, its road and transportation systems are comprehensive, and its industrial base, particularly the newly constructed facilities in Yanbu and Jubail, is state-of-the-art. Numerous agencies for the development of new businesses are attempting to distribute capital to every sector of the economy. Elaborate university and college systems are educating Saudi citizens in a broad range of disciplines, and thousands of local schools and training programmes are facilitating the transfer of technology to the economy's private and public sectors.

While oil revenues have allowed the creation of a large stock of capital assets, the Kingdom faces a number of unique business development opportunities and problems. Urbanisation happened faster than anyone in the Kingdom expected, causing extreme inflation in housing and foodstuffs in the late 1970s and early 1980s. Saudi Arabia has become the world's premier rentier state, and is almost completely dependent on imported labour. Government initiatives have led to agricultural and private sector economies financed through subsidy programmes. Some officials and scholars claim that liberal financing programmes are a conduit through which oil revenues are redistributed to the population. Others believe these policies link business revenues and asset values more closely to aid and grant programmes than to corporate efficiency. In agriculture, Saudi farms are currently more highly mechanised than farms in Indiana and Nebraska, but costs in terms of water and fertiliser usage are high. This is the topic of Salah Al-Suhaibani's chapter in this volume (Chapter 10).

While its growth in capital assets is obviously unmatched among nations in the region, perhaps in the world, the Kingdom's business development has been accompanied by difficult periods of social adaptation. New technology has had to prove itself to be an enhancer of Islamic mores. This has usually not been difficult, but it has sometimes been very costly. Training programmes have often had to reflect the employment choices of Saudi citizens rather than the needs of the manufacturing and producing sectors. Service-based industries, for example, dominate the patriot employment market, possibly reflecting ancient traditions in Arab culture that tend to promote service-oriented mercantilism in the Saudi socioeconomic hierachy.[1] The constant choice of middle-skilled, service- and retail-oriented employment by Saudi entrants into the job market has forced the community to maintain its reliance on foreign labour in many industrial sectors.

It is important to realise that the Kingdom's culture, its attachment to the Islamic faith, its history as a Bedouin society and other factors such as its oil endowments, population concentration, arid climate and sparse solid natural resources make traditional Western theories about business development inapplicable to Saudi Arabia. Each Five Year Development Plan saw the introduction of new ideas about the optimal relationship between government and industry. What has generally developed is a partnership approach where the government provides assistance in financing and planning, and businesses provide entrepreneurial skills, management acumen and marketing expertise. The resulting structure is a mixture of public planning and private enterprise initiatives, although weighted more towards the former than the latter. While the economic system recognises the value of private initiatives, it is also acutely aware that private sector efforts to date have happened within a framework of state guidance and leadership.[2]

Economic activity in Saudi Arabia is dominated by the extraction, refinement and exportation of oil. In addition to oil's direct impact on income, changes in oil prices and their effect on the national budget play a central role in the Kingdom's industrial production. Government investment, as a percentage of total investment, increased by just under 7 per cent in 1960 to 42.9 per cent in 1965, 53.3 per cent in 1970 and 72.6 per cent in 1980. By

1985, however, due to a growing number of privately owned manufacturing concerns, the public sector's share in the nation's industrial investment declined to 54.2 per cent.[3] Government consumption makes up the majority of domestic orders, thus encouraging domestic investment activity in the economy's non-oil and private sectors.

Growth in the private sector is also largely dependent on the provision of services to government. The current rate of private sector growth is low, though increasing, in large part due to the declining profitability of oil. In 1981/82 oil accounted for 64.7 per cent and non-oil products for 35.3 per cent of GDP; of the non-oil component, the government accounted for 44.2 per cent and the private sector for 55.8 per cent. In 1987 oil accounted for 26.4 per cent and non-oil products for 73.6 per cent of GDP; of the non-oil component, the government accounted for 39.2 per cent and the private sector for 60.8 per cent. Thus the private sector accounted for only 19.2 per cent of the total economy in 1981/82, when oil prices were low, and for 44.7 per cent in 1987.[4] The private sector's share of gross fixed capital formation increased from 72.2 per cent in 1988 to 73.2 per cent in 1989. Gross fixed investment in the non-oil private sector also increased by 3 per cent between 1989 and 1990. This reinforced the leading role the private sector is expected to play in the business development process in the 1990s.[5]

Despite the government's dominant position in the economy, it is committed to the emergence of a market-oriented economy. One of the main problems is that many of the revenues that the private sector received in the 1970s and 1980s were reinvested in Europe or the United States. An enormous pool of private capital has accumulated abroad. At the end of 1990 commercial banks in Saudi Arabia had transferred into foreign assets an excess of SR 93 billion over their foreign currency liabilities.[6] Billions more have left the country through the remittances of foreign workers, the largest amounts going to Egypt, Jordan and Palestine, and to advisors from the United States and Europe.

In response the government has decided to refocus its funding on credit extension and away from grant and aid allotments. Both specialised lending agencies, which in the past 15 years have provided close to SR 225 billion of low-cost loans to industry,[7] and the commercial banks will have more influence over the credit distribution system in the coming years. In recent years, Saudi Industrial Development Fund subsidies have decreased significantly in favour of stricter commercial credit rationing for the private sector. This change in policy is designed to force domestic investors, who were accustomed to high rates of return on investment through subsidy dependency during the rapid period of growth from 1974 to 1982, to operate as profit-maximising enterprises.

With this change in focus has come a growing realisation that the private sector should be directly involved in writing development plans,[8] mainly because it is felt that business people can best help to remove the remaining constraints that are hindering entrepreneurial investment. Some barriers to business development are found in the attitudes of private sector managers. Many Saudi business owners seem unable to adopt a long-term approach to management, preferring instead to work with immediately profitable contracts for ministries and agencies. In addition, accountancy laws and lending are often ignored by small business owners and managers, and the absence of a well-defined bankruptcy infrastructure discourages banks from taking on long-term risk exposure with small businesses.[9]

According to Soufi and Mayor, mixed signals are also present in the administration of free market policies.[10] The government has generally let the private sector determine its own local long-run comparative advantages. However this *laissez-faire* approach means that counterproductive internal competitive environments have developed. For instance there were already three firms making refrigerators in 1988 when it was announced that three more would begin production by 1995. The early factory owners feel that they are not receiving the promised market protection. Askari argues, however, that the government feels that protection from foreign competition is enough and that increased domestic production will enhance competition and result in more competitive exports.[11]

Saudi Arabia's business development process in the 1990s is characterised by declining government funding of private sector consumption, making it difficult for some firms to maintain liquidity. But the increasing efficiency and productivity of most Saudi manufacturers should move primary consumption away from public sector dependence and towards business-to-business market. The Saudi experience clearly illustrates that merely owning abundant foreign exchange does not automatically make the business environment thrive. If over the next twenty years the problems discussed are alleviated by proper incentives, the Saudi Arabian economy will possess a strong private sector.

This collection of essays is an introduction to the recent historical and contemporary operation of the Saudi Arabian business environment. The text is divided into two parts. Part I chronicles the planning efforts that have supported business development and the market maturation process in recent decades. Of particular note is the role of government investment objectives in helping business owners to overcome economic and social barriers to development. Part II examines industry-specific barriers and opportunities. These chapters evaluate the policies discussed in earlier articles, but they also discuss the means by which businesses overcome problems. Issues addressed include export strategy, human resource constraints, private sector dependency, growth in agriculture and small business development. Each chapter provides readers with the background necessary to understand the Saudi business environment. It is an economy unlike any other in the world, simultaneously vast in its demands and wealth, and yet limited by its shortage of human and material resources.

Finding Americans who can effectively and readily interpret the nuances of Saudi Arabia's business environment is difficult. For this reason many of the articles in this collection have been rewritten or cowritten by J. W. Wright Jr and a Saudi scholar in order to ensure that they display a uniquely Saudi perspective. Wright wrote several of the chapters on the basis of recent dissertations by named contributors. Chapter 5 on the managerial environment was rewritten from lectures given by Al-Garawi and Schmidt. In Chapter 6 Khasshogi and Vaughn discuss Saudi Arabia's impact on regional labour migration and trade. Dr Al-Aali's article on the import–export trade (Chapter 11) was also reworked by Wright. Three chapters, those by Drs al-Hajjar and Presley (Chapter 9), Abdel-Rahman and Metwally (Chapter 12) and Al-Suhaibani (Chapter 10), are updated versions of previously published articles.

The editors and contributors wish to emphasise their feeling that the constant attention to Saudi's oil industry has overshadowed the real progress made in the Kingdom's non-oil business sector. Although we discuss the role of oil revenues in financing development projects, we are not natural resource economists. By taking this perspective, *Business Development in Saudi Arabia* is a unique project that presents original information to the Western reader about Saudi commerce. It will add significantly to industrialised nations' understanding of their largest Arab trading partner. More importantly, we hope our essay will stimulate new discourses on East–West commerce and cooperation.

References

1. Charles Issawi, *An Economic History of The Middle East and North Africa* (New York: Columbia University Press, 1982), p. 10.
2. Robert E. Looney, *Saudi Arabia's Development Potential* (Massachusetts: Lexington Books, 1982), p. 36.
3. Robert E. Looney *Economic Development in Saudi Arabia: Consequences of the Oil Price Decline* (Connecticut: JAI Press, 1990), p. 2.
4. Hossein Askari, *Saudi Arabia's Economy: Oil and the Search for Economic Development* (Connecticut: JAI Press, 1990), p. 124.
5. Saudi Arabian Monetary Agency, *Annual Report* (Riyadh: SAMA, 1990), p. 86.
6. The Economist Intelligence Agency, *Country Report* Saudi Arabia, no. 3, 1991, p. 5.
7. Henry T. Azzam, *The Gulf Economies in Transition* (New York: St. Martin's Press, 1988), p. 4
8. Wahib A. Soufi and Richard T. Mayer, *Saudi Arabian Industrial Investment, An Analysis of Government-Business Relationships* (New York: Quorum Books, 1991) op. cit., p.19.
9. Azzam, op. cit., p. 42.
10. Soufi and Mayer.
11. Askari, op. cit., p. 127.

Part I

The History of Business Development in Saudi Arabia

Before tackling the intricacies of the new business environment in Saudi Arabia, it is necessary to study private sector development issues from an historical perspective. This is the task of the chapters in this section, each of which chronicles the planning efforts that have become the basis for business development in Saudi Arabia.

1 Culture, Royalty and Saudi Business Development: A Historical Perspective

J. W. Wright, Jr

There are only a few states in the world where the ruling families have so much influence on the nation's business economy as they do in Saudi Arabia.[1] Indeed there may be none. In this chapter we will look at the attitudes and cultural perspectives of the five Saudi Kings towards business development activities as they can be seen in the Kingdom's economic development plans. My goal is to combine the information found in academic historical texts about these monarchs and the data provided in their development policies to illustrate their roles in building an emerging and effective private business sector.

THE INITIATION OF AN OIL ECONOMY

Saudi Arabia today would be an entirely different place if oil revenues had not been available to finance development construction. The mainstream production of oil in the 1940s changed the complexion of the Kingdom's government, its industry and its role in the Arab region's economic structure. In addition, with the coming of oil production came the intrusion of Western industry. Foreign companies created many of the successes in the Saudi economy, but their ambitions in world oil markets often left them little time to consider the development agendas of local businesses. The Arab-American Oil Company (Aramco), although certainly more benevolent than most of its British and French counterparts, had near monopolistic control over the Kingdom's early business environment.[2] Aramco even served as the country's primary envoy to the international business community throughout the reigns of the first two Kings.[3]

Saudi monarchs, however, have always recognised the power of oil, especially King Abdul-Aziz. He was well aware that the increasing use of oil in the world's industrial production placed Saudi Arabia in a position of considerable international influence. Commercial and political advisors knew it too, and when President Roosevelt and Prime Minister Churchill came to visit, it was oil that was used to secure political leverage in Washington and London. At the time, Abdul-Aziz's clout allowed the country to stay free of colonialist intervention in the affairs of his local governments. Many political analysts believe that his ability to withhold commercial contracts from American and European oil companies allowed him to delay the Western governments' support of the annexation of Palestinian territories.[4]

In 1935 world oil consumption peaked at 1.8 million barrels a day; by the end of the Second World War consumption had risen to 7.8 million barrels a day; and by 1957 it had reached 18.3 million barrels a day.[5] The Middle East region too was dependent on oil consumption. In 1954 69 per cent of total energy consumption was oil-based,[6] primarily because other natural resources were either nonexistent or underdeveloped in the region.[7] At that time, 70 per cent of the world's known oil reserves were in Iraq, Kuwait and Saudi Arabia (Saudi Arabia holding the lion's share).[8] Consequently oil production and petroleum revenues rose dramatically in the postwar period, as shown in Table 1.1. Oil production commenced in Qatif and Ain Dar in 1945, with a combined production of 170 000 barrels a day. Similar wells were opened throughout the country's eastern region, and the first offshore well was opened at Safaniya in 1951. By 1953 137 wells were producing 845 000 barrels of oil daily. In 1954 the refinery at Ras Tanur, which in 1944 had a 50 000 barrel a day capacity, was expanded so that it could process two million barrels a day.[9]

During the 1950s Saudi Arabia operated ostensibly as an oil economy, with few other sectors producing products for export. King Abdul-Aziz was most interested in alleviating the burdens his people had felt from taxes and pilgrimage fees. He was intent on recycling oil revenues into social support systems such as hospitals and schools, feeling that these facilities were necessary before long-term development could take place. Therefore he

Table 1.1 Saudi Arabian oil production and petroleum revenues, 1944–54.

Year	*Production (barrels)*	*Oil refined in country (barrel)*	*Saudi gov'ts oil revenue ($US)*
1945	21 311 000	2 953 623	4 820 000
1946	59 944 000	29 297 101	13 500 000
1947	89 852 000	39 065 060	20 380 000
1948	142 853 000	45 086 139	31 860 000
1949	174 009 000	46 269 619	66 000 000
1950	199 547 000	38 364 333	112 000 000
1951	277 963 000	58 107 534	155 000 000
1952	301 861 000	62 204 161	212 000 000
1953	308 294 000	74 559 673	166 000 000
1954	347 000 000	79 800 000	260 000 000

promoted the expansion of a near-unilateral business economy based on oil royalties. In 1953, 90.3 per cent of government income came from oil taxes and sales. As a result of reinvesting petrodollars into the oil industry's infrastructure, revenues increased to $340 million in 1960, $663 million in 1965 and $1.2 billion in 1970. By 1973, two decades after Abdul-Aziz's death, the refinery at Ras Tanur had the capacity to load 439 000 barrels of oil per hour, nearly ten times the amount that could be refined in 1953.[10]

In the 1960s, however, the Saudi government grew concerned about the concentration of the Kingdom's industrial base.[11] It was also concerned about meeting the increasing needs in the local market for refined oil. Demand for refined petroleum had grown at an annual rate of nearly 14 per cent in the Middle East,[12] and at a rate of 27 per cent in Saudi Arabia since 1950.[13] The increased use of the Suez Canal by oil tankers also indicated a need to find more effective ways of transporting oil to ports on the Red Sea. In response to these developments, expansion of refining capacity at Ras Tanur continued and the Trans-Arabian pipeline was built to carry oil from Saudi's Eastern Province to the Mediterranean shores near Sidon. The pipeline was completed on 25 September, 1950,[14] and by December it carried oil equivalent in quantity to that of 72 oil tanker runs through the Suez Canal.[15]

Still, the Kingdom needed new ports with industrial capacity on both coasts. The fact that two pipelines were being built through Iraq,[16] and that plans to expand the Suez Canal were under way, threatened Saudi's strategic position in the West. Moreover the threat of war could not be ignored. If the Suez Canal were to close, or if the pipeline were to be destroyed, Saudi Arabia's revenues from shipments through the Western Region could be decimated. Simultaneously, in the Eastern Region the need for new ports was strengthened by the higher demand for oil from Asian nations.

During King Saud's years on the throne, oil revenues continued to provide 90 per cent of total government revenue.[17] While sales of crude oil may have provided the capital needed to finance economic development, it was the planned economic restructuring that took place during King Faisal's rule that paved the way to rapid business growth.[18] King Faisal's accession to the throne in 1964 brought a new Saudi government attitude about business development and private sector activity.[19] He believed major offensives were needed to develop a 'dual economy'[20] whereby the Kingdom could (1) regain control of its natural resources and exploit them more effectively for industrial development, and (2) support private sector development of traditional industries through small business initiatives.[21] In one generation the new King wanted to shake the Kingdom's dependence on foreign industrial intervention and become a member of the world's power elite.[22]

King Faisal's strategy for developing a private-sector-led economy was threefold. First, government spending would be redirected towards projects that served dual infrastructure and security functions, that is, the construction of industrial-grade roads, military-ready civilian airports and state-of-the-art communications and medical systems. The government would underwrite the initial cost of these projects and reserved the right to use them in times of military incursion. These facilities would be primarily used, however, to enhance the abilities of businesses to form and produce products and transport them for export. The percentage of government expenditure for industrial projects rose to $350 million in 1969, three and a half times the amount spent ten years earlier, and gross fixed capital formation in the non-oil sector rose by an average of 18.68 per cent per annum between 1964 and 1969.[23]

Second, industrial construction would focus on refined oil products such as petrochemicals, fertilisers and lubricants. Because of its oil reserves, Saudi Arabia has distinct comparative advantages for producing petroleum-related products. Until facilities were built to refine oil by-products into lubricants, materials and so on, the Kingdom would lose both cost savings domestically and revenues from international export sales.

Third, government planners were to depend less on the advice of oil executives and more on the advice of hired consultants, namely the US Army Corps of Engineers and the United States–Saudi Arabian Joint Commission for Economic Cooperation. The US Corps of Engineers became the dominant force in Saudi Arabia's development planning efforts during the Faisal era because of strategic concerns that too many of the Kingdom's infrastructure systems were being commercially controlled. Saudi officials felt they could purchase a broader-based transfer of technology through the Corps, which was more able to design facilities serving both civilian and security interests.[24] Although the Corps took charge of many military assignments, its primary role was to support a planning process concerned with private sector business development.[25]

Step one of King Faisal's plan hinged on the restructuring of the oil industry. The main export at the time was crude oil, but some Saudi planners believed profit margins were being lost to the designs of foreign oil companies. Initiatives were taken to assure the sales of more refined oil products that carried higher price premiums on world commodity markets. The budget for refinery expansion and petrochemical development was significantly increased and the share of value-added oil products in GDP rose at a higher rate than those of non-oil value-added products (traditional and handicraft products). The ratio of oil to non-oil products in value-added GDP is shown in Table 1.2.[26] This situation would change as steps were taken to develop agriculture, cottage manufacturing and industrial cities. The first step was to harness the potential of oil and regain control of Aramco.[27] The Saudi government owned 25 per cent of Aramco's shares by 1973, 60 per cent by 1976 and 100 per cent by 1980.[28]

Table 1.2 Ratio of oil to non-oil products in value added GDP

Year	*Total*	*Value-added GDP* *Non-oil*	*Oil*	*% of Value-added oil GDP*
1965	10258	7297	2961	28.87
1966	11976	7457	4519	37.74
1967	13843	7712	6131	44.29
1968	14657	7764	6893	47.03
1969	15974	8705	7270	45.51
1970	17399	9293	8106	46.59

Faisal's next objective was to strengthen the government's control of the planning, policy and regulatory processes. The Kingdom's first efforts at planning came in 1958 with the establishment of the Economic Development Committee, which was replaced by the Supreme Planning Board in 1960.[29] It was not until this board had been replaced by the Central Planning Organization in 1965 (currently the Ministry of Planning) that fully integrated budgets were regularly published. The budget plans written between 1966 and 1970 are the precursors of the often quoted and highly successful Five Year Development Plans, which began in 1970.[30] As a result of these plans, oil revenues fuelled development programmes and propelled the country's transformation into a modern industrial society.[31]

One of the more striking examples of institutional maturation during the era of King Faisal is found in the financial sector. Six banks operated in the Kingdom prior to the establishment of the Saudi Arabian Monetary Agency in 1952: the Netherlands Trading Company, Banque de l'Indochina, Bank of Palestine, National Bank of Pakistan, British Bank of the Middle East, and the Egyptian Bank.[32] The Netherlands Trading Company held the Saudi government's foreign currencies. The Saudi-owned National Bank of Commerce was the first Saudi bank approved by the King in 1952,[33] followed by Bank of Riyadh, which was licensed by the Al-Suwailim, Abu Dawoud and Bin-Zagr families in 1957.[34] The Saudi Arabian Monetary Agency (SAMA) was created in 1952 to function as a licensing bureau, a gold and silver exchange, holder of the government's monetary reserves and regulator of banks operating in the Kingdom.[35] However SAMA could not print money or handle local currency until 1959 and it had little control over the country's financial system.[36]

Under the leadership of King Faisal the government began to bring the Saudi financial system under its control. The impetus for many regulations came from the near failure of the Bank of Riyadh in 1964. SAMA intervened by buying a 38 per cent stake in the bank. In an effort to avert further bank failures, SAMA's powers were considerably extended in 1965. In 1966 the Banking Control Code was issued, which significantly constrained and standardised the operation of banks in the Kingdom.[37] As a result of this standardisation, the licensing of banks grew rapidly in the late 1960s and the early 1970s.

By the time Prince Khalid became King in 1975 there were 14 Western-styled banks operating in the country. In addition a number of specialised banks were created under Faisal to improve the distribution of funds earmarked for business development. The Saudi Arabian Agricultural Bank was founded in 1964; the Public Investment Fund was chartered in 1971; and the Saudi Credit Assistance Bank Act was signed in 1973. The Saudi Industrial Development Bank was established in 1974 with the objective of providing medium- and long-term loans for up to 50 per cent of the total requirements of the new industrial construction, expansion, modernisation and renovation projects. The Real Estate Development Fund (REDF) also made its first loans in 1974, intent on resolving the shortage of private and public housing.[38]

King Faisal's planning model also included a comprehensive training component, which was in the directives he gave to the United States-Saudi Arabia Joint Commission for Economic Cooperation when it was founded in 1972. By providing consulting services to the Kingdom's industries and institutions, the Joint Commission was made responsible for organising cooperative efforts in the fields of accounting, agricultural banking, demographic planning, industrial construction, labour training, scientific research and water management. The Joint Commission was unique both in format and influence as it focused almost entirely on government employees.[39]

In essence, the development of Saudi Arabia's economic and financial systems is based on King Faisal's mandates aimed at expanding financial services to the business community. This means the current economic system has developed in less than 30 years; the progress made in this short period of time is impressive. We will look next at the direction of planning and development finance in each of the Five Year Development Plans.

AN ANALYSIS AND DESCRIPTION OF THE FIVE YEAR DEVELOPMENT PLANS

The formal publication of the Five Year Development Plans began in 1970 with a plan that paled in the face of the economic conditions following the 1973 Arab–Israeli war. The OPEC oil embargo had dramatically changed the structure of world oil markets and significantly elevated Saudi Arabia's position as an international trading partner. The oil revenues that followed in 1974 dwarfed any expectations that had been written into the original plan, with government revenues rising from $2744 and $4340 million in 1972 and 1973, to $22 574 and $25 676 in 1974 and 1975.[40] During the pre-plan period (1965–70) expenditure had only been 24 800 million riyals.

King Khalid did not inherit a failed planning system but a system that had derived great benefit from the national planning effort, and he had at his disposal King Faisal's network of development financing institutions.[41] More importantly, the first plan provided the Kingdom with a three-pronged strategy that guided the second and third plans: (1) the diversification of the economic structure through growth in manufacturing, (2) the short-term mobilisation of foreign human resources and the long-term training of an indigenous workforce, and (3) the expansion of oil-related businesses. The projected expenditures for the first, second and third plans are shown in Tables 1.3–1.5.

It is clear that the goal of the first plan was to improve the efficiency of the business environment through infrastructure development. Next to expenditure on defence and administration, the country's road and communications systems received highest priority. Much of the defence expenditure also went to facilities that served dual commercial and military functions. Human resource development was the next priority, followed by the con-

Table 1.3 Financial appropriation for the first Five Year Development Plan, 1970–75 (million Saudi riyals, constant 1970 prices)

Appropriations	*Amount*	*Percentage*
Administration	7717.4	18.6
Defense	9555.0	23.1
Human Resource	7377.7	17.8
Health and Social Affairs	1921.1	4.7
Public Utilities	4572.3	11.1
Transport and Comm.	7474.5	18.1
Industrial Construction	1098.5	2.7
Agriculture	1467.7	3.6
Trade and Services	127.3	0.3
Total	41 313.5	100.00

Table 1.4 Financial appropriation for the second Five Year Development Plan, 1975–80 (milliion Saudi riyals, constant 1970 prices)

Appropriations	*Amount*	*Percentage*
Administration	38 179	7.7
Defence	78 196	15.7
Human resources	80 124	16.1
Health and social affairs	33 213	6.7
Infrastructure development	112 945	22.7
Agriculture	2 900	2.3
Economic resources Development	92 135	18.5
Other	60 578	10.3
Total	498 270	100.00

struction of a public utility system. Given the turbulent years in which it operated and the changing of leadership in the Kingdom, the first plan was surprisingly successful in constructing infrastructure.[43]

The oil price hikes in 1974 allowed the government to attack infrastructure problems more aggressively in the second plan, which operated on a budget six times that of the first plan. The percentages of total expenditure set in the first plan for the

Table 1.5 Financial appropriation for the third Five Year Development Plan, 1975–1980 (million Saudi riyals, constant 1970 prices)[44]

Appropriations	*Amount*	*Percentage*
Administration	31 400	4.0
Defence (not listed separately)	–	–
Human resources	129 600	16.6
Health and social affairs	61 200	7.8
Infrastructure development	249 100	31.8
Agriculture	2 270	2.9
Economic resources development	261 800	33.4
Other	47 330	3.5
Total	782 700	100.00

development of human resources and health and social development did not change substantially. Defence expenditure, although it increased significantly in dollar terms, declined as a percentage of total expenditures. The 'Other' account consisted of external assistance, emergency funds and reserves. During this period a number of human social welfare goals were reached, including the provision of free medical services, subsidised housing and expense-free education and training.

Most obvious was the increase in infrastructure expenditure in the second plan, including spending on economic resource development – the construction of resource-related product processing facilities (agriculture, mining, natural gas). Physical construction for industry represented over 40 per cent of the budget. Added to this was the amount spent on military construction and loans for agricultural development. Sixty-five per cent of funding was directed into business-oriented, real-estate-intensive projects. This expenditure allowed the private sector effectively to exploit Saudi Arabia's comparative advantage in natural resources and transportation. Investment in foreign business property is not included here.

King Khalid's plan was to intensify efforts towards manufacturing diversification. At the heart of his efforts was the creation of industrial cities at Yanbu and Jubail. Both cities are based near major refining facilities where natural gas, which had previously been lost when oil was extracted, was gathered and used to fuel the manufacture of hydrocarbons and petrochemicals. Included in the plans were oil-related plants capable of producing fertilisers, methanol, ethylene, polyethylene, ethylene glycol, butane, liquefied gas, plastics and sulfur. Non-oil-related production facilities were planned for aluminium, beverages, cement, food processing, electric consumer goods, tyres and vehicles.

As the second plan unfolded, structural developments began to reflect King Khalid's objectives. As Tables 1.6 and 1.7 illustrate, all sectors increased their output during the 1975–80 period, but the infrastructure and manufacturing sectors far outperformed the more traditional sectors. The construction sector's share of non-oil GDP doubled, and there was a strong movement away from employment in agriculture, with some 15 per cent of the labour force leaving agriculture and moving into jobs in the manufacturing sector.[45] Non-oil production increased dramatically from less than 2 per cent in 1963 to 27.4 per cent in 1973 and 33.9 per cent in 1980.

Table 1.6 Sectoral share of non-oil GDP,[46] annual percentage growth rate of real output

Sector	*1975/1980*	*1980/1985*
Producing sector		
Agriculture	5.1	6.2
Mining	4.6	–16.5
Manufacturing	9.8	6.9
Utilities	21.9	18.6
Construction	15.8	–0.9
Sub total	6.9	–7.2
Service sector		
Trade	22.7	9.2
Transport	19.3	7.1
Finance	14.0	4.4
Other services	3.3	1.9
Government	–	6.4
Sub total	15.1	6.9
Total non-oil sector	14.8	6.4
Oil sector	4.8	–14.2

Table 1.7 Sectoral share of GDP, 1973–90 (percentages)

Sector	*1973*	*1975*	*1980*	*1985*	*1990*
Producing sectors:					
Agriculture	1.0	0.9	5.4	4.1	4.8
Mining	0.2	0.4	1.0	1.1	1.1
Manufacturing	1.4	1.9	4.8	7.3	10.4
Petrochemicals	–	–	–	–	2.6
Utilities	–	0.1	0.2	0.5	0.5
Construction	8.4	12.9	32.3	23.5	17.7
Sub total	11.0	16.2	41.8	36.5	37.1
Service sector:					
Trade	2.7	4.9	13.2	15.8	15.5
Transport	3.2	5.6	11.8	13.0	14.3
Real estate	–	–	8.0	7.1	6.2
Finance	2.9	3.7	3.4	5.0	6.6
Other services	1.1	1.5	3.9	4.5	4.6
Government	6.5	5.9	17.5	18.1	15.7
Sub total	16.4	21.6	58.2	63.5	62.9
Total non-oil sector:	27.4	37.8	34.8	60.2	57.1
Oil sector	72.6	62.2	65.2	39.8	42.9
Total	100.0	100.0	100.0	100.0	100.0

The third plan represented a basic continuation of the objectives set forth in the first and second plans, including a major emphasis on infrastructure and resource development. Funding for expansion in these two sectors increased by 149 per cent to a combined total expenditure of SR510 billion. Continuing emphasis was placed on the building of facilities that could be used for defence and civilian purposes, although it was more specific in promoting growth in the non-oil sectors. Construction of ports and airports was deemphasised as more attention was paid to building industrial facilities. This was evident to an even greater extent after Crown Prince Fahd became King in 1982.

As the mandates of the third plan were implemented, distinct structural changes became apparent. The construction industry declined as a percentage of non-oil-sector growth, while non-oil manufacturing rose from 5 per cent to 7 per cent. More importantly, the service sector took on a somewhat new identity, gaining 64 per cent of the economy's output in 1985. With road and port facility expansion nearing completion by 1985, the transportation sector saw significant growth, as did commercial trade (wholesale and retail), and the real estate sector established itself as a viable industry. Predictably, the service and manufacturing sectors became the big winners in terms of employment transfer, with another 10 per cent of the workforce moving into non-agricultural jobs.

Three main sets of structural changes became apparent.[47] First, the level of growth in the economy was being driven by or was concentrated in manufacturing and services. However it must also be noted that the consumption demand in the non-oil sectors were directly tied to government financing and procurement programmes. Up to 75 per cent of private sector spending was supported by government-financed assistance, grants, loans or subsidy programmes. While the non-oil sectors were becoming more efficient, and were therefore less directly affected by oil sales, they were indirectly influenced by oil prices when the government financing programmes went into retrenchment.[48]

The second structural change manifested itself in the interaction between the various sectors of the economy, especially the traditional sectors. By the beginning of the fourth plan agriculture had become much more productive and Saudi Arabia became a grain exporter. At the same time employment in agriculture declined by 25 per cent, while the service sector grew to account for 73 per cent of the Kingdom's patriot employment.[49] The redistribution of jobs by sector is shown in Table 1.8.

Third, with increased industrial diversification the direction of production changed from large industrial projects to small and medium-sized manufacturers. With this trend a strong middle-class political–economic element in the community developed in Saudi Arabia.[50] From a development point of view, economic reliance on this new business class will create significant finance gaps, but it also should create substantially more jobs. It is important to remember that small businesses are riskier to operate and more difficult to finance, and studies show that there is a high level of managerial inefficiency among Saudi's entrepreneurial class.[51]

Table 1.8 Employment by economic activity, 1979–80 and 1984–85

	1979–80 *(Thousands)*	*(%)*	*1984–85* *(Thousands)*	*(%)*	*Growth rate* *(%)*
Producing sectors:	1424.2	47.0	2067.2	46.5	7.7
Agriculture	545.6	18.0	617.4	13.9	2.5
Other mining	2.3	0.1	5.1	0.1	17.3
Other manufacturing	170.4	5.6	411.4	9.3	19.3
Utilities	67.0	2.2	147.4	3.3	17.1
Construction	638.9	21.1	885.9	19.9	6.8
Service sectors:	1157.7	38.3	1844.6	41.5	9.8
Trade	323.1	10.76	556.1	12.5	11.5
Transport	180.0	6.0	303.4	6.8	11.0
Finance	51.8	1.7	136.3	3.1	21.4
Other services	602.8	19.9	848.8	19.1	7.1
Government*	399.4	13.2	469.1	10.5	3.3
Non-oil sectors	2981.3	98.5	4380.9	98.5	8.0
Oil Sectors	44.7	1.5	65.1	1.5	7.8
Total	3026.0	100.0	4446.0	100.0	8.0

* Excludes non-civilian employment and includes daily wage workers not classified as civil servants.

King Fahd's fourth plan (1985–90) marked a decided change in the Saudi government's position on business development.[52] Because infrastructure construction was ostensibly complete and most medium-sized and large industrial firms had received liberal financing, it was decided that the private sector needed to be weaned away from the public sector.[53] As Looney puts it, 'the basic messages of the [fourth] plan is that the state, having made massive investments in establishing a modern infrastructure, wants the private sector to shoulder more of the investment burden, and eventually to emerge as the main force in the economy'.[54]

At the beginning of the fourth Five Year Development Plan there were about 2000 producing entities in the Kingdom. Those firms supplied only 50 per cent of the goods consumed, even though they were physically capable of supplying all of the Kingdom's demand for consumer goods.[55] The crux of the problem lay in the fact that facilities were not being managed for maximum efficiency. Too often business owners could not distinguish between cash flow generated from profits and money received from government subsidies.[56] Imports had fallen by 28 per cent during the third plan, and it was hoped that they would fall another 30 per cent by 1990. Because of these circumstances the fourth plan emphasised the efficient use of the Kingdom's new facilities.[57] Planned overall growth during the period was only 4 per cent, but growth in agriculture was placed at 6 per cent, in the financial sector at 9 per cent and in private sector manufacturing at 15.5 per cent. Table 1.9 shows the actual growth rates by sector.

Unfortunately oil revenues did not rebound as hoped and spending levels fell during the term of both the third and fourth plans. Even after the budget cuts, government spending remained consistent with the strategies underlying the plan. Construction allocations declined in all areas, with industry and infrastructure suffering the largest cuts. Spending on social services was maintained and King Fahd's commitment to developing a more highly skilled indigenous workforce kept funds for human resources intact. These two areas of the budget seemed to be immune to cutbacks under the fourth plan. In terms of

Table 1.9 Sectoral growth rates (per cent)

	1987	*1988*	*1989*	*1990*
Agriculture	15.4	12.1	11.3	9.0
Mining	3.3	–2.5	18.3	65.2
Oil and gas	3.4	–2.6	18.7	66.7
Other mining	–1.9	1.8	5.0	6.0
Manufacturing	10.9	3.7	15.5	11.0
Petroleum refining	18.0	–2.3	15.5	11.0
Other manufacturing	.9	8.0	7.1	7.5
Public utilities	30.0	6.0	5.0	6.0
Construction	–2.3	–5.0	1.4	2.0
Financial and business services	2.9	9.2	7.1	–2.5
Defence	–2.0	3.2	4.8	10.0

Source: Ministry of Finance and National Economy, Kingdom of Saudi Arabia.

growth, the agriculture sector showed the most resilience on a sectoral basis. Tables 1.10–1.12 show intended and actual expenditure during the plan, and Table 1.13 shows the sectoral growth rates from 1987–90.

Table 1.10 Development expenditure during the fourth Five Year Development Plan

	Expenditure structure		
	Third plan		*Fourth plan*
	Plan (%)	*Actual (%)*	*Plan (%)*
Spending category:			
Economic resources development	31.3	21.4	26.1
Human resources development	21.3	22.2	27.1
Health and social services	10.0	12.4	17.9
Transport and communications	22.7	24.7	15.4
Municipalities and housing	14.7	19.3	13.5
Total: development agencies	100.0	100.0	100.0

	Expenditure level			
	Third plan		*Fourth plan*	
	Plan	*Actual*	*Plan*	*% Change from third plan, actual*
*Spending category:**				
Economic resources development	190.7	120.4	130.7	+8.6
Human resources development	129.6	124.3	135.3	+8.8
Health and social services	61.2	69.6	89.7	+28.9
Transport and communications	138.6	139.1	76.9	–44.7
Municipalities and housing	89.3	108.9	67.4	–38.1
Total: development agencies	609.4	562.3	500.0	–11.1

* Amounts are in current prices.
Source: Ministry of Planning, Kingdom of Saudi Arabia, *Fourth Development Plan* (Riyadh, 1985), p. 73.

Table 1.11 Budget allocations by sector (1401/2–1408/9) (Saudi riyals)

	(1984/5)	*(1986)*	*(1987/8)*
Human resource development	23 962	23 725	23 388
Transport and communications	16 500	11 934	9 493
Economic resource development	14 434	8 439	5 888
Health and social development	14 830	11 094	10 806
Infrastructure development	6 670	4 300	3 555
Municipal services	11 890	8 100	7 017
Public administration, government utilities etc.	31 582	31 266	25 058
Lending to credit institutions*	9 300	3 590	590
Local subsidies	8 343	6 800	5 325
Non-defence expenditure	137 511	109 248	91 120
Defence and security	64 085	60 752	50 080
Total planned expenditrue (SRm)	201 596	170 000	141 200

*Includes transfer to Saudi Fund for Development.
Sources: Various SAMA and government publications.

The fifth plan has the same fundamental objectives as the fourth plan, although efforts towards education and training have obviously intensified. For the first time, human resource development is receiving the highest level of funding, 18.7 per cent of the total budget and 35 per cent of the non-government budget. This reflects King Fahd's intention to support the managerial needs of the private sector and the training needs of government agencies. It is also a call by the king for the economy he heads to move away from public sector dependence towards private sector activity.[58] Therefore, as the oil sector's proportional contribution to GDP fell to 25 per cent in 1991, the burden of creating new employment opportunities began to fall more squarely on the shoulders of small and medium-sized businesses. These firms still account for 80 per cent of the Kingdom's total employment.

Finally, another current aim of the government is to operate with balanced budgets. The 1990s have thus far been turbulent years for Saudi Arabia, and highly volatile oil markets plus the costs of war have made it difficult for the government to meet this goal. The budget deficits of the 1980s can be resolved, however, by replacing public sector spending with private sector incentives.

Table 1.12 Summary of employment distribution by economic activitiy, 1970–90 (per cent)

Activity	*1970*	*1975*	*1980*	*1985*	*1990*
Manufacturing (including petroleum and refining) and other	5.4	3.0	4.0	9.3	12.7
Mining, quarrying and other (including oil and natural gas)	2.3	3.0	2.6	1.6	2.5
Commerce and other sectors*	8.3	13.0	14.3	15.8	15.0
Services**	1.4	1.3	1.2	22.2	22.9
Transport, communications and storage	18.1	19.0	19.1	6.8	7.0
Social and community services, including education and health	4.7	5.5	8.2	–	–
Utilities	1.1	1.2	1.3	–	–
Subtotal	41.3	46.0	50.7	55.7	60.1
Public administration	5.5	5.5	7.0	10.5	10.6
Construction	12.8	20.5	25.4	19.9	13.8
Agriculture, forestry and fishing	40.4	28.0	16.9	13.9	15.5
Total	100.0	100.0	100.0	100.0	100.0

* Such as trade, restaurants and hotels. ** Such as insurance, real estate and business services.

As a result of the planning efforts of Kings Faisal and Khalid, and due to the continued leadership of King Fahd, Saudi Arabia has moved rapidly into a new era of business activity. Today, established industrial cities stand in places that were once small villages. Goods are now regularly produced by Saudi companies that twenty years ago were considered luxuries. Education and health care are free to all citizens. The country's infrastructure and defence systems are second to none. And, the country has set itself on a course that will allow it successfully to create freer and more diversified internal markets.

It is important to acknowledge the major progress that has been made in the Saudi market in just twenty years. The number of factories will top 3000 by the end of the current Five Year

Table 1.13 Saudi Aramco's projected long-term expansion programme for the years 1991–2003

1991–94	Safaniya	Tie-in platforms	265
	North Hawiyah	GOSP-2 and 3[1]	160
	North Hawiyah	Water injection project	300
	Marjan	Completion	175
	Zuluf	WCHF[2]	320
1992–95	South Hawiyah	GOSP-4	160
	South Hawiyah	Water injection	150
	N.A.[3]	Sea-water pump station	100
	Uthmaniyah	GOSP-5	150
1993–96	Berri	Gas lift and other work	460
	Safaniya	Gas lift	325
	Sadaniya	Tie-in platforms	300
1994–97	Berri	WCHF	40
	Khursaniyah	Four projects	235
	Harmaliyah	Three projects	110
	Abu Hadriya	Five projects	195
	Qatif	GOSP-1	55
1995–98	Qatif	WCHF	40
	Safaniya	GOSP-3	340
	Safaniya	Gas-lift	250
	Safaniya	Tie-in platforms	300
	Manifa	Five projects	1,130
1996–99	Manifa	Four projects	1,100
	Suluf	Three projects	255
1997–2000	Haradh	Four projects	440
	Khurais	Water injection	300
1998–2001	Haradh	Four projects	640
	Qatif	Five projects	305
	Qatif	Gas-lift	40
1999–2002	Shaybah	Seven projects	2,200
2000–2003	Shaybah	Five projects	760
	Qatif	Five projects	550

Notes
1. Gas–oil separation plants.
2. Wet-crude handling facilities.
3. Not applicable.

Source: Compiled from *Middle East Economic Digest* (MEED) June 1990, p. 23.

Development Plan. Growth in the manufacturing and service sectors has redefined the Kingdom's employment activity. Product services have become the leading employer of all sectors, including government and military. Commercial trade has doubled employment opportunities since 1970. Manufacturing has risen from 3 per cent of total employment to 12.7 per cent. Agriculture, the largest employer in 1970, has declined by 25 per cent in terms of the number of people employed. Agricultural production, however, exceeds 10 per cent of non-oil GDP.

This does not mean that planning in the oil sector will be put into the background. Aramco too is planning to expand its operation. Oil sales will continue to be the Kingdom's main source of revenue and foreign reserves, and oil-related projects will continue to have priority in the future. The new economic order has, however, reduced the country's dependency on a single source of production, and reduced the chance that sudden swings in oil prices could affect the economy as a whole. More importantly, the new Saudi economy has shown that countries wanting to keep their traditional institutions intact can support rapid industrial modernisation.

Notes and References

1. This chapter is an adaptation of a lecture delivered by J. W. Wright, Jr at the Smithsonian Institution on 18 May, 1993. A collected edition of these lectures is available in Abdulaziz Al-Sweel and J. W. Wright, Jr, *Saudi Arabia: Tradition and Transition* (Michigan: Hayden-McNiel, 1993), pp. 27–68.
2. Peter R. Odell, 'The Significance of Oil', in J. E. Peterson (ed.), *The Politics of Middle Eastern Oil* (Washington, DC: Middle East Institute, 1983), pp. 5–13. Also see in this collection, Edith Penrose, 'International Oil Companies and Governments in the Middle East', pp. 14–31.
3. Another book that discusses changes in world oil markets during the 1930s, 1940s and 1950s is Irvine H. Anderson, *ARAMCO, the United States, and Saudi Arabia: A Study of the Dynamics of Foreign Oil Policy 1933–1950* (Princeton: Princeton University Press, 1981.) In addition to presenting information that is repeated in several of the sources I have consulted for this lecture, Anderson addresses frankly American 'strategies' for exerting influence on the Saudi monarchy for military and commercial reasons. Political commentaries about plans to manipulate Saudi government policy can be found in Dean Achison, *Present at the Creation: My Years at the State Department* (New York: W. W. Norton, 1969), and Leonard Mosley, *Dulles: A Biography of Eleanor, Allen, and John Foster Dulles and Their Family Network* (New York: The Dial Press, 1979).

4. 'The Private Files: The United States, Israel and Saudi Arabia', documentary of the Public Broadcasting System, previewed at the Brookings Institute, October 1992.
5. Leonard M. Fanning, *The Shift of World Petroleum Power Away from the United States* (Pittsburgh: Gulf Oil Corporation, 1958), table 4, as cited by Albert Y. Badre and Simon G. Siksek, *Manpower and Oil in Arab Countries* (Beirut: American University of Beirut, Economic Research Institute, 1960), p. 5.
6. George Lenczowski, *Oil and State in the Middle East* (Ithica: Cornell University Press, 1960), p. 42.
7. Michael Hanifee, 'The Impact of Oil on Saudi Arabia', address given at Washington College, Chestertown, MD, 1992.
8. *Petroleum Press Service*, vol. xxv, no. 8 (1958), p. 258, as cited by Badre and Siksek, op. cit., pp. 7–8. For similar verification see, Arabian-American Oil Company, *Aramco Handbook: Oil and the Middle East* (Dahran: Aramco, 1968), p. 78.
9. The table presented here is a compilation of information found in Benjamin Shwaran, *The Middle East, Oil and the Great Powers* (New York: Praeger, 1955), pp. 344–50. It is interesting to note that while the construction of this refinery was indeed expensive, approximately $82 million, it is estimated that the cost to Aramco were recovered from the sale of oil to the US Navy in 1944 and 1945.
10. Richard F. Nyrop, Beryl L. Benderly, Laraine N. Carter, Darrel R. Eglin and Robert Kirchner, *Area Handbook for Saudi Arabia* (Washington DC: US Government Printing Office, 1974), pp. 265–7.
11. Niel H. Jacobi, *Multinational Oil* (New York: Macmillan, 1974), p. 62.
12. Lenczowski, op. cit., p. 42.
13. Shwadran, op. cit., p. 363.
14. Aramco, op. cit., pp. 148–50.
15. Proposals for pipelines running from the Arabian Gulf to the Mediterranean were not new. Harold Ikes, then US petroleum administrator for war, had announced plans for Aramco and the Petroleum Reserves Corporation to build such a pipeline in 1943. The Navy Petroleum Board also entered an agreement with the Petroleum Reserves Corporation to buy oil pumped through this pipeline. It is not clear how much of the planning came from the Pentagon and how much from the corporations. The plan was never implemented, apparently at the recommendation of the Truman Committee in 1944. For more details see, Leonard M. Fanning, *American Oil Operations Abroad* (New York: McGraw-Hill 1947).
16. Details of the initial planning of these pipelines can be found in Raymond F. Miksell and Hollis B. Chenery, *Arabian Oil: America's Stake in the Middle East* (Chapel Hill: The University of North Carolina Press, 1949), pp. 55–68.
17. This assertion is verified in several previous citations. Additional tables on the Saudi Arabian Budget Estimates (1948–58) are found in George A. Lipsky, *Saudi Arabia: Its Peoples, Its Society, Its Culture* (New Haven: HRAF Press, 1959), pp. 317–19. According to the data presented by Lipsky, oil revenues and customs and port receipts (oil duties) financed 86 per cent of the government's total expenditure in 1953 and 100.3 per cent of expenditure in 1958. The ratio of oil revenue to expenditure was

88 per cent from 1948–58. These percentages did not change significantly until after Faisal's rule as king. Lipsky also discusses 'domestic trade' in Saudi Arabia during the 1940s and 1950s, see Chapter 17.

18. Naief M. Almtairi, 'The Development Process and its Relation to Oil Revenues and Dependence on Imported Labor Market in Saudi Arabia', PhD diss., University Texas at Austin, 1991.
19. Roger Webster, 'Bedouins Take the Fruit of Progress', *The Middle East Journal*, vol. 91 (May 1982), pp. 41–58.
20. Mukhtar M. Ballool, 'Economic Analysis of the Long-term Planning Investment Strategies for the Oil Surplus Funds in Saudi Arabia: An Optimal Control Approach', PhD diss., University of Houston, 1981.
21. Edmond Y. Asfour, 'Prospects and Problems of Economic Development in Saudi Arabia, Kuwait, and the Gulf Principalities', in Charles A. Cooper and Sidney S. Alexander (eds), *'Economic Development and Population Growth in the Middle East* (New York: Elsevier, 1927), pp. 367–98.
22. Almtairi, op. cit., p. 123.
23. Lipsky, op. cit., pp. 319–20; Asfour, op. cit., pp. 371, 379.
24. Andrew M. Evans, 'The U.S. Corps of Engineers in Saudi Arabia: The Civilian-based Programs', address at Washington College, Chestertown, MD, 1992. See also John T. Greenwood, 'Diplomacy Through Construction: The U.S. Corps of Engineers in Saudi Arabia' (Washington, DC: Corps of Engineers, 1984), pp. 1–3; Joan F. Kibler, 'Phase Out in Saudi Arabia', *Military Engineer* (March – April, 1989); Victoria Hammond, 'Constructing the New World Order: The Case of the U.S. Army Corps of Engineers in Saudi Arabia', Middle East Studies Association Occasional Paper Series (Tempe: Middle Eastern Studies Association, 1991), p. 2.
25. Ambassador Twinam, address on the 'Activities of the United States Army Corps of Engineers in Saudi Arabia', hearing before the Committee on Foreign Affairs, 96th US Congress, House Foreign Affairs Committee, 25 June 1979. See also *The Saudi Arabian Programs* (Winchester, VA: Public Affairs Division of the Middle East Division, Corps of Engineers, 1985). This point is also discussed by Marc Brewen in 'The U.S. Corps of Engineers in Saudi Arabia: The Military Programs', address to Washington College, Chestertown, MD, 1992.
26. Ballool, op. cit., pp. 33–5. Figures are quoted at current prices in millions of Saudi riyals.
27. An important note is that the percentage of exports that were oil-based did not change during this period. The percentage of oil products compared with total exports was 99.7 per cent in 1960, 99.7 per cent in 1962, 99.2 per cent in 1964 and 99.8 per cent in 1966. The composition of oil-based exports changed and consisted of more refined or value-added products: Ibrahim M. Al-Awaji, 'Bureaucracy and Society in Saudi Arabia', PhD diss., University of Virginia, 1971, p. 87.
28. Joy W. Viola, *Human Resource Development in Saudi Arabia: Multinationals and Saudization* (Boston: International Human Resource Development Corporation, 1986), p. 33.
29. Al-Awaji, op. cit., pp. 147–63. Several outside teams were hired to evaluate the planning needs of the Saudi government, including teams from the Ford Foundation, the United Nations and the US Federal Reserve. This indicates the level of King Faisal's commitment to professional planning.

30. David Edens and William Snavely, 'Planning for Economic Development in Saudi Arabia', *Middle East Journal* (Winter 1970), p. 18.
31. Almtairi, op. cit., p. 113.
32. Listed in order of their entry into the Kingdom.
33. Rodney Wilson, *Banking and Finance in the Arab Middle East* (New York: St. Martin's Press, 1982), p. 280.
34. Sadig A-H. Malki, 'Institutional Inconsistency: A New Perspective on the Role of the State in Development: A Case Study of Saudi Arabia', PhD diss., Washington University, 1991, pp. 47–50.
35. Ramon Knauerhase, *The Saudi Arabian Economy* (New York: Praeger, 1975), pp. 238–9.
36. Jaber A. Al-Shamrani, 'The Impact of Economic Development on the Financial System in Saudi Arabia', MA Thesis, Colorado State University, 1990, pp. 7, 25–31. Al-Shamrani's comments are supported by Rahji el-Mallakh, *Saudi Arabia: Rush to Development* (London: Croom Helm, 1982), and A. N. Young, *The Making of a Financial Giant* (New York: New York University Press, 1983).
37. Malki, op. cit., p. 48, and Al-Awaji, op. cit., pp. 143–62.
38. Al-Shamrani, op. cit., pp. 22–5.
39. The early project agreements included agricultural bank management and training, comanaged by the Saudi Arabian Agricultural Bank and the US Farm Credit Administration; the Ministry of Agriculture and Water, comanaged by the Ministry of Agriculture and Water and the US Department of Agriculture; desalination and hydroponics, comanaged by the Saudi Arabian Saline Water Conservation Corporation and the US Department of Agriculture; executive management development, organised through cooperative arrangements with US private industry; university development, designed for King Faisal University with the US Department of Education; manpower development and vocational training, comanaged by the Ministry of Labor and the US Department of Labour; audit administration and training, comanaged by the Saudi Arabian General Control Board and the US Department of Treasury; and central procurement and supply management. These agreements reflected important challenges faced by King Faisal and his planning administrators when they wrote the first and second Five Year Development Plans. At each point in the discussion, the common denominator was the orderly transfer of technology.
40. Saudi Arabian Monetary Agency, Research and Statistics Department, Statistical Summary, 1985, pp. 68–71.
41. The following discussion of the Five Year Development Plan is an amalgamation of my own research and information taken from Almtairi's, Ballool's and Fozan's dissertations. Other references will be cited directly.
42. Ministry of Planning, Third Development Plan, 1980–5, p. 88.
43. Central Planning Organization, First Development Plan, 1970–5, p. 43.
44. John A. Shaw and David E. Long, *Saudi Arabian Modernization: The Impact of Change on Stability* (New York: Praeger, 1982), p. 12.
45. John R. Presley, *A Guide to the Saudi Arabian Economy*, (New York: St. Martin's Press 1984), p. 12.
46. Third Development Plan, 1990, pp. 12–20.

47. Henry T. Azzam also discusses the transitory stage of development for Saudi Arabia and the other Gulf States in *The Gulf Economies in Transition* (New York: St. Martin's Press, 1988).
48. Robert Looney, *Economic Development in Saudi Arabia: Consequences of the Oil Price Decline* (JAI Press, Greenwich, 1990), pp. 88–89.
49. Presley and Westaway, pp. 100–1.
50. Mark Holler and Nadav Safran, *The New Middle Class and Regime Stability in Saudi Arabia* (Cambridge, MA: Center for Middle Eastern Studies, Harvard University, 1985).
51. Bandar al-Hajjar and John R. Presley, 'Managerial Inefficiencies in Small, Manufacturing Businesses in Saudi Arabia: A Constraint Upon Economic Development', Proc. of the 1991 British Society for Middle Eastern Studies Conference (London: University of London, 1991). Also see Robert Looney, pp. 111–36.
52. Fouad Al-Farsy provides detailed analysis of the fourth plan in two books. See: *Modernity and Tradition: The Saudi Equation* (London: Kegan Paul International, 1990), pp. 159–64; and *Saudi Arabia: A Case Study in Development* (London: KPI Limited, 1986), pp. 162–77).
53. John R. Presley, 'Private Sector Holds Key to Goals of Fourth Plan', *Middle East Economic Digest Special Report: Saudi Arabia* (July 1985), p. 96.
54. Looney, p. 281. A substantial amount of carryover of projects from the third plan were completed in the period of the fourth plan. Looney, p. 36. The biggest infrastructure projects had been completed and the factories at Yanbu and Jubail were quickly coming on line. There were no major projects in the fourth plan. For example, the Ministry of Agriculture and Water had by 1988 built 180 dams, only 11 more were planned over the periods of the fourth and fifth plans. Almtairi, 140.
55. 'Saudi Arabia: Revival Predicted in the Early 1990s', *Middle East Economic Digest* (December 20, 1986), p. 60.
56. J. W. Wright, Jr, 'Accounting in Saudi Arabia: Imperative Questions for the 1990s', Proceedings of the 1992 British Society for Middle Eastern Studies Conference (St. Andrews: St. Andrews University, 1992), pp. 636–44. The problems of overzealous financing in an economy without a standardized and regulated accounting industry are also addressed in Bandar al-Hajjar, John R. Presley, and J. W. Wright, Jr, 'Structural and Attitudinal Impediments to Efficient Capital Distribution in Saudi Arabia's Islamicizing Economy: Implications for Financial Sector Training'. Proceedings of the World International Seminar on Islamic Economics at the World Bank (International Institute for Islamic Thought, Washington, DC, forthcoming).
57. R. J. A. Gazzard, 'Physical Planning in Saudi Arabia: aspects of plan preparation, approval and review', Proceedings of the 1992 British Society for Middle Eastern Studies Conference, (St. Andrews: St. Andrews University, 1992), pp. 372–87.
58. John Presley, Tony Westaway, and John Sessions, 'Saudi Arabia: Problems of Economic Development in the 1990s', Proceedings of the 1992 British Society for Middle Eastern Studies Conference (St. Andrews: St. Andrews University, 1992), pp. 602–18.

2 Business Policy in an Era of New Prosperity: Strategic Investment Planning from 1970 to 1985

J. W. Wright, Jr, with
Muhktar M. Ballool[1]

This chapter is mainly concerned with the investment strategy problems that faced Saudi Arabia in recycling the petrodollar surpluses that accrued to the Kingdom in the 1970s as a result of price hikes following the OPEC embargo. The embargo happened in the midst of the country's first Five Year Development Plan, drastically altering the implementation of that plan and setting up completely new dynamics for writing investment objectives into the next two plans. Several issues complicated the investment planning process, not least of which was the fact that until then, and indeed until the late-1980s, the economy of Saudi Arabia had depended on a single, exhaustible natural resource as its sole source of income. In 1970, 80 per cent of Saudi GDP and 99.83 per cent of the government's revenues were earned through the sale of oil and related gas by products.[2] The government's dependency on oil sales forced planning officials to question whether the exhaustible resources were being depleted too rapidly.[3]

Several other major complicating factors surrounded the early investment planning process. The first was that planning the optimal use of surplus oil funds was neglected until 1964. Written planning policies did not surface until 1970, and even then the data on the Kingdom's economy was highly unreliable. Moreover the idea that the Kingdom would have more money than it could spend was an alien concept prior to 1973. Therefore the country's planning officers did little to integrate the oil surplus funds into the development planning process prior to 1970, or in their writing of the first plan. This chapter, following a brief historical review, will primarily focus on the investment objectives presented in the second and third plans.

Before moving on, however, it is necessary to emphasise that both the production rate of oil resources and their per unit value are determined by the political environment in the Kingdom. In addition, Saudi Arabia's strategic position geographically, geologically and religiously make it vulnerable to external political interference. The labelling of the oil production rate as an endogenous factor or a market-driven variable might be fine academically, but because of the Kingdom's and the world's political realities, hypothetically convoluted models based on this assumption had no real value for Saudi planners in the late-1960s and mid-1970s. Dealing with so many unknown variables made long-term investment planning an exceedingly difficult task.

BACKGROUND NOTES

The Kingdom of Saudi Arabia occupies about nine-tenths of the Arabian peninsula, an area somewhat larger than Alaska and Texas combined. Oil-rich deposits have become, since the 1940s, the Kingdom's chief source of revenue. The government is patriarchal, with a nearly absolute ruler who is assisted in his duties by a council of ministers. Prior to 1970 more than half of the Saudi population were Bedouin nomads,[4] and most villagers worked as subsistence farmers or herders raising wheat and livestock.[5]

The Kingdom's monetary and economic systems in its first four decades were based on the principle of a mixed economy. On the one hand, like any other free market economy the Kingdom's money demand was based on derived demand, the primary force being the demand for consumer goods, capital goods and government services. However, the similarity between the Saudi economy and other free market economies ended at that point. In other free economies, money requirements are predominantly determined by the demand for consumer goods, and to a lesser degree by government expenditure. In Saudi

Arabia, however, from the 1940s until the 1980s government expenditures constituted more than 90 per cent of aggregate demand. This situation came about because the Kingdom's oil revenues accrued directly to the government.

The transfusion of money into the arteries of the Saudi economy was mainly dependent upon the government's ability to spend money, and to a lesser degree upon private sector activity. Prior to 1970 gross domestic product (GDP) in Saudi Arabia relied on three sectors: agriculture, the government services sector and the oil sector. The non-oil sector (mainly agriculture) at that time employed 90 per cent of the population but had very little influence on efforts to raise the average levels of national income or financial liquidity. The Kingdom still exhibited most of the production characteristics of an underdeveloped country.[6] The general standard of living was low, there was widespread malnutrition, a low life expectancy and high infant mortality (even though the population growth rate at the time was 2.1 per cent),[7] and the majority of the population were illiterate.

The country's internal situation has changed considerably since the 1973 oil embargo, when the rate of investment expenditure internally and externally rose dramatically. The impact of increased oil revenues in Saudi Arabia were twofold. The direct regional effects were improved infrastructure, job creation, the construction of industrial complexes and the addition of more oil by-product refining facilities. The latter is most apparent in the eastern provinces, where most of the oil is produced. The heavy industrial complexes that were planned for Yanbu and Jubail are examples of how the government planned to recycle oil revenues into the non-oil economy.

The major indirect impact of oil production was the sharp rise in monetary income. The origin of this income – oil sales – had little bearing on how the government planned to reinvest the capital for domestic expansion. A triangular interrelationship of oil revenues, government expenditure and political decision making determined the actual use of the new domestic and foreign reserves. Expenditure was determined by revenue and the price of imported capital, consumer and technology transfer goods. The major constraints on expenditure were fears about domestic inflation and the lack of a large domestic labour force.

Still, in light of the government's recognition of these opportunities and constraints, it can be said that the early business development strategy followed prior to 1965 was imprecise and informal in nature. It was essentially a planning model that revolved around royal preference based on intuition, and on political and economic consideration of optimal capital allocation.

GOVERNMENT PLANNING

The need for public economic planning in Saudi Arabia arose from the urgent need to invest the available oil resources in the most efficient manner. As Edans and Snavely put it, the priorities included, 'such things as reducing the level of unemployment, raising average per capita income, expanding exports to reduce the balance of payments gap, attaining a favorable real growth rate, maintaining reasonable price stability, and providing favorable stimulation and incentives for the private sector of the economy'.[8] In 1966 criteria for formal planning were developed. First, it was essential to have a government planning agency headed by a non-political administrator, preferably a well-trained economist. Second, a well-trained technical staff would be assigned to the planning agency. Third, the planning agency would have an informal organisational structure that would make it possible for the staff to operate under efficient and flexible circumstances. Fourth, a department of statistics would be developed to provide an extensive body of accurate statistical data to be used in the planning process. The fifth priority was to construct and implement formal business development programmes that integrated goals ranging from infrastructure construction to educational proficiency. Finally, the plan should be approved by all the ministries that would be involved in its implementation.

During the five-year pre-plan period (1965–70) actual expenditure was only SR 24 800 million, compared with SR 74 336 million during the first Five Year Development Plan, SR 688 500 million in the second plan and SR 784.4 million in the third plan. In 1970 the Central Planning Organisation was created to coordinate government spending, and it issued the first plan that year. This plan set the direction and tone for the next fifteen years of development planning. Its goals were forthright: to minimise dependence on oil exports as the principle source of revenue, to build a national industrial and social services infrastructure, to reduce dependence on imported consumer goods and to develop an indigenous labour force. The first plan, however, had little resemblance to the path of development the Kingdom actually followed, due to the speed at which it became outdated after the oil embargo of 1973. The budgets for all the plans are presented in Table 2.1.

The Central Planning Organisation was transformed into the Ministry of Planning with the beginning of the second Five Year Development Plan. In the second plan construction was the main goal, followed by maintaining a high rate of economic growth by developing economic resources, maximising earnings from oil in the long term, conserving depletable resources, reducing economic dependence on the exportation of oil, developing human resources through education, raising the standards of health care, fostering social stability, and building up the physical infrastructure of the country.[9] The plan stressed diversification of the economy by encouraging the expansion of agriculture, industry and mining, with an emphasis on the petrochemical and mining industries, in which the Kingdom enjoys a comparative advantage. It stressed the need to provide free education and training to all people in the Kingdom, and it emphasised the goal of building free medical facilities across the country. The plan aimed to provide gainful employment to all citizens and to maintain a dignified minimum standard of living for all citizens.

To these ends the government intended to make sure that essential goods, especially staple food items, would be available at stable and reasonable prices, subsidising prices if necessary. Investment in family housing would be arranged on easy terms and constructed through government initiatives for those with limited incomes. In addition, 'while the government of Saudi Arabia will uphold the market system and encourage the private sector to play a fundamental role in the accelerated growth and development of the country, it will take all necessary measures to make the market system conform to the larger social interests of the country'.[10]

The notable difference between the second plan and the third is the budget rather than the direction. Fearing that world oil prices

Table 2.1 Summary of the Saudi Arabian Five Year Development Plan allocations

Items or Sectors	*First plan 1970–75*	*% of 1st plan*	*Second plan 1975–80*	*% of 2nd plan*	*Third plan 1980–85*	*% of 3rd plan*	*Fourth plan, 1985–90*	*% of 4th plan*	*Fifth plan 1990–95*	*% of 5th plan*
Natural resources	–	–	–	–	–	–	–	–	24.5	3.3
Productive sectors	–	–	–	–	–	–	–	–	45.4	6.0
Economic resources	14 742.0	35.7	92 135.0	18.5	261.8	33.5	130.7	13.1	–	–
Human resources	9 258.8	22.4	80 123.9	16.1	129.6	16.6	135.3	13.5	141.1	18.7
Social development	*	*	33 212.8	6.7	61.2	7.8	89.7	9.0	87.2	11.6
Infrastructure	–	–	112 944.6	22.7	249.1	31.8	144.4	14.4	97.9	13.0
Subtotal	24 000.8	58.2	318 416.3	64.0	701.7	89.7	500.1	50.0	396.1	52.6
Administration	7 714.4	18.7	381 779.2	7.7	31.4	4.0	70.2	7.0	102.1**	13.5
Subsidies and reserve	–	–	63 478.2	12.7	499.6	6.3	117.3	12.0	–	–
Defence and security	9 550.0	23.2	78 156.5	15.7	–	–	312.5	31.0	255.1	33.9
Subtotal	17 272.4	41.8	179 813.9	36.0	81.0	10.3	500.0	50.0	357.2	47.4
Total	41 273.2	100.0	498 230.2	100.0	782.7	1000.0	1000.0	100.0	753..3	100.0

* A residual figure.
**Allocation for this sector to be included in human resources for first plan.
Sources: *EIU*, no. 1 (1990), pp. 1–29; Development Plan, 1970–75; *MEED*, (May and July) 1975, p. 8.

might not remain stable, the government dramatically accelerated the level of infrastructure and industrial construction. Funding for real estate projects was ten times that of the first plan and three times that of the second plan. The plan placed new emphasis on developing Saudi manpower in order to replace foreign workers to the maximum extent possible, which was somewhat at odds with the increased labour demands inherent in the plan's increased construction expenditure. The goal of replacing foreign labour, however, was not met during the plan's term. The third plan maintained the overall theme of diversifying national income by creating new government-sponsored income-producing enterprises. In addition, the Saudi International Bank was formed in 1975 to facilitate government-directed investment in foreign corporate shares and foreign government debt and income instruments.

Both plans recognised without qualification that the most important economic determinant was oil production and that no sector of the economy would be effectively developed without shared oil revenues. At the beginning of the third planning period, political–economic considerations included relatively stable crude oil prices, but there was also an economic crisis in the West brought about by high rates of inflation causing exorbitant interest rates and high unemployment in the Americas and Europe, particularly in the United Kingdom and the United States. Saudi officials led discussions at OPEC meetings on the dangers of adding to the West's economics crisis by curtailing oil production. Saudi was in favour of raising oil prices at a rate consistent with inflation, and it encouraged price unity between OPEC members at the 1980 annual meeting in Algiers. Sheik Yamani, then minister of petroleum, indicated that Saudi Arabia would give preference in oil sales to nations willing to supply modern industrial technology to the Kingdom.

With the Saudi agenda for commercial diversification and technology transfer made clear both internally and externally, the question that arose most often was how much of its oil surpluses should the government invest in Western money markets and how much should it spend on asset creation in domestic markets. Certainly investing all of its surpluses in either of these options was not rational. The decision was made to divide the money between capital expenditure and expenditure on development, consumption and defence, and to invest part of the revenues in foreign income-producing assets. Infrastructure construction would be aimed at facilities that would produce revenues for the government and the private sector on a long-term basis, allowing for a three to five year lead time.

While the first three plans harboured the same basic and ambitious goal of creating an independent economic base, there was a limit to what could be achieved. The Saudi government therefore decided in the third plan to invest more heavily in just a few key industries, mainly agriculture, basic metals and petrochemicals, rather than continuing to start numerous costly projects before others had been completed. The decision to concentrate on these three business sectors took place in 1978.

The Eastern Province in particular saw massive economic activity, including construction of a huge industrial complex at Jubail, a 750 mile gas pipeline and energy plant, a solar energy plant,[11] new ports and airports[12] and a host of fertiliser, lubricant, petrochemical and plastics plants. The western province city of Yanbu was to receive investment at a similar level, although with fewer oil-dependent industries.

The third plan also stipulated for the first time that the government, while encouraging entrepreneurship in a free market environment, would pursue its goals through planned economic activity. The main force of this planned economy would be government spending, which still accounted for the vast majority of national consumption. In addition the government would allocate funds and offer incentives as stimuli for private sector activity, which became a major emphasis in the fourth plan. Moreover a definite directive in the third plan was for the modernisation of backward areas and underdeveloped regions, indicating a learning curve directed towards balanced regional economics.

INVESTMENT BY SECTOR

Agricultural production in the Kingdom initially centred around cereals, vegetables, potatoes, dates and other fruits. The agricultural sector had two distinctive characteristics. First, while it contributed less than 2 per cent of GDP, 60 per cent of the population in 1975 was engaged in subsistence agriculture or nomadic livestock herding.[13] Second, agriculture remained the least developed sector of the economy. The chief factors limiting the scale of agricultural production were the scarcity of water, primitive irrigation techniques, low incentives for large-scale or corporate investment, inadequate mechanization and inadequate road and marketing facilities between farms and markets.

A third complicating factor was created by the oil boom itself. The increase in oil wealth was detrimental to agricultural development in that it encouraged rapid urbanisation without any increase in agricultural productivity. Oil wealth also encouraged a pattern of consumption in favour of imported over domestically produced goods.[14] In 1980 the country still imported two thirds of its food products. The result was that there was a net decline in the contribution of agriculture to GDP. The annual growth rate of the agricultural sector measured at constant 1970 prices was the lowest of all sectors of the economy.[15]

The extent to which agricultural production could be increased would be determined by increased efficiency in the use of water. In turn, better education and training for farmers and basic reforms in farming techniques had to be introduced to all rural areas where farm production took place, particularly in the south west region where there was much family-subsidised farming and a labour surplus. The government resolved in the second and third plans to provide the necessary land grants, infrastructure and distribution channels to private entrepreneurs who were willing to adopt mechanised agriculture with economies of scale.[16]

The non-oil mineral sector received much attention in the 1970s. In addition to petroleum, the Kingdom has huge natural gas reserves and promising deposits of metallic and non-metallic minerals.[17] The leading non-oil resource is natural gas. Table 2.2 presents the known and estimated amounts of natural gas between 1970 and 1980.

It was decided during the second plan period to use Saudi gas to fuel power at Yanbu and Jubail. Therefore the majority of facilities at the Jubail industrial site were designed to use gas-powered heating units. Yanbu's industrial complex, which is further from the gas deposits than Jubail, is less dependent on natural gas, but the need for gas-powered heating prompted the

Table 2.2 Natural gas, 1970–80 (billion cubic feet)

Year	*Reserves* *Known*	*Estimated*	*Total output* *Produced*	*Flared*
1970	50 220	68 234	728.4	523.8
1971	50 904	76 344	899.8	702.6
1972	52 638	89 962	1164.9	969.6
1973	56 126	107 378	1564.1	1341.7
1974	60 963	105 481	1670.7	1380.3
1975	62 290	109 514	1396.3	1035.3
1976	86 000	111 214	1680.9	1390.2
1977	88 190	120 470	1870.1	1910.3
1978	91 210	121 500	2321.7	2101.4
1979	94 120	150 478	2543.9	2253.7
1980	98 620	NA	NA	NA

Sources: *Oil and Gas Journal*, 1972 to 1979; Aramco, *Annual Report*, 1974 to 1978; *Facts & Figures*, 1973 to 1978.

government to construct a 750 mile pipeline between the two cities. The problem in 1980 was that there was simply not enough bottling and storage capacity to handle the amount of gas made available by increased oil production. With an average oil/gas ratio of 500 hundred standard cubic feet per barrel of oil produced, the Kingdom was forced to burn off 2253.7 billion cubic feet of gas for every 2543.3 billion cubic feet stored. Therefore the third plan emphasised investment in new gas refining units at Jubail and Ras Tanura and the construction of a gas pipeline system throughout the Kingdom.

As stated above, other mineral resources also showed commercial promise. Saudi Arabia has the largest endowment of non-oil mineral deposits in the Gulf region.[18] In addition to these minerals, large deposits of clay, limestone, gypsum, glass sand, cement and marble exist in the mountainous regions, offering alternative sources of national income.[19] At the beginning of the third plan, however, the level of mining activity was negligible compared with the country's non-oil mineral needs and its potential for natural resource exploitation. Accordingly the third plan included extensive investment in mineral exploration and the mining of both metallic and non-metallic minerals. The list of minerals cited in the second plan for possible exploitation included copper, zinc, gold and lead in Al-Amarand Jubal Sayid, Massene and Nugrah; iron in Jebal Idsas, Wadi Sawawin and Wadi Fatima; nickel in Wadi Qatan; phosphates in Thaniyat and Turaif; uranium in Thaniyat and potash in Turaif.[20] A major iron ore mining facility capable of extracting an estimated 1.5 billion tons of medium and low grade (45–50 per cent) iron ore was to be constructed just west of Jeddah, and it was planned to prospect for uranium deposits.

The industrial structure of the Saudi economy was, at the time the third plan was written, characterised by a number of problematic rigidities. First, there was the relative immobility of productive factors between consumer-goods and capital-goods industries and between agriculture and manufacturing. Inefficient labour exchange systems, transportation and communication facilities, and ill-organised capital markets all contributed to this immobility. Second, too many small-scale capital goods producers were using obsolete, often primitive, plant and equipment. Cheap labour imported from Egypt, India, Palestine and Yemen was often used instead of much more efficient machinery, especially in construction and mining. This situation was also apparent in farming, food processing and weaving. Third, the gap between skilled and unskilled labour had the effect of discouraging the installation of 'streamlined' plant and equipment. The government's recognition of these constraints prompted it to pledge massive aid and subsidy funding to help the private and public sectors build and develop efficient non-labour intensive industrial and manufacturing facilities.[21]

In manufacturing, a list of priorities was drawn up with respect to aid and grant money. These funds were intended not only to facilitate the construction of industries, but also to reduce the nation's overall construction and development costs. Public sector investment went mainly to hydrocarbon-based industries, that is, fertiliser production, steel fabrication, and energy refining. The next to benefit from public sector spending were producers of other construction-related manufactures such as concrete and plastics; followed by businesses such as those processing consumer products, including canning and packaging. These priorities, each obviously linked to the other, aimed to cut the Kingdom's dependency on imported construction materials such as concrete, lubricants and steel reinforcement materials, and to reduce prices of locally grown, produced and packaged consumer goods.

To facilitate this development King Khalid established the publicly held Saudi Basic Industries Corporation (SABIC) to promote large-scale industrial projects, mainly in petrochemistry, iron, steel and aluminum smelting. SABIC was also to enhance the petroleum refining, gas gathering and mineral transition activities that were assigned by the government to the General Petroleum and Mineral Organisation (Petromin), which is fully owned by the government. In addition to these bodies, a separate government organisation was created to develop a system of integrated grain silos and flour and feedmeal products. The third plan included a projected expenditure of almost SR 900 billion on priority industries in Jubail and Yanbu alone.[22] More funds were earmarked for similar projects through local and regional funding and lending operations.

The proposed plants in these two industrial complexes included a $2 billion petrochemical complex at Jubail with a capacity to process 721 000 tons of ethylene and 324 000 tons of styrene a year; a $1.6 billion plant in Yanbu that could produce 495 000 tons of ethylene, 220 000 tons of low density polyethylene, 220 000 tons of ethylene glycol and 100 000 tons of high density ethylene (Table 2.3); a $680 million steel mill at Jubail; and a multi-billion dollar gas-gathering and processing system, able to handle the processing and transportation of six billion cubic feet of a gas per day. Funding was also provided to build a 750 mile east–west pipeline (mentioned earlier) between Jubail and Yanbu to transport gas from the eastern province to Red Sea factories and ports. Most of these new facilities were to be constructed either by the private sector through direct capital contributions, or funded through the sale of shares once the various companies became operational.[23]

The major constraint on these industrial construction plans was the lack of labour in the Kingdom. The uniqueness of Saudi Arabia's situation of having a surfeit of capital resources to invest in capital-intensive construction or in sophisticated imported technology while at the same time having almost no domestic labour force to attend to the actual implementation of

Table 2.3 Volume and types of production of SABIC's first-phase industrial programme

	Annual production capacity (metric tons)
Petrochemical projects:	
Ethylene	2 000 000
Low density polyethylene	708 000
High density polyethylene	196 000
Ethylene glycol	650 000
Styrene	
Ethylene dichloride	454 000
Crude industrial ethanol	281 000
Caustic Soda	377 000
Methanol	1 300 000
Polyisoprene	300 000
Fertiliser:	
Urea	1 000 000
Metallurgical projects:	
Iron and steel	
Sponge iron	800 000
Steel billets	850 000
Reinforced wire rods and bars	1 000 000
Aluminum	
Aluminum ingots	225 000

Source: Saudi Arabian Monetary Agency, *Annual Report*, (Riyadh, 1979) p. 80.

these plans, cannot be overstated. The problem was compounded by the inability of the institutional framework to support and sustain massive doses of technology without imported managerial labour and large numbers of foreign unskilled labour. All these factors proved extremely costly and threatened to cripple the successful implementation of the third plan.

Both the second and third plans, but especially the latter, made provisions for accumulating huge capital reserves to invest in foreign countries. Saudi Arabia's international monetary reserves were matched only by those of West Germany, the United States and Japan. These plans called for overseas investment to grow and diversify throughout the 1980–85 period. Prior to the third plan most of the Kingdom's foreign reserves had been retained in a fairly liquid form, but it was decided to make more permanent investments with surplus oil revenues in the 1980s. These investments ranged from loans to foreign governments and international organisations such as the International Monetary Fund and the World Bank (where Saudi received directorships) to direct investment in various private and public enterprises in Europe, Japan and the United States. In addition, loans to other developing countries were made in return for easy market entry or oil sales contracts. Examples of these investments include short-term loans to the governments of Brazil, Congo, Egypt and longer-term loans, ranging from 12 to 20 years, (the United Kingdom) to the International Monetary Fund and the World Bank. It was not unusual for these loans to be as large as $750 million at 8.5 per cent interest, for example the loan the Kingdom made to the World Bank in 1975. Loans were also made to the foreign private sector – AT&T, for example, borrowed $100 million from the Saudi government in 1975.

The Saudi International Bank (SIB), of which SAMA owned 50 per cent, had been making foreign investment decisions since its founding in 1975 and was given the authority to expand its operations during the period of the third plan.[24] Key SIB investments have centred around international financial institutions. Major SIB holdings at the turn of the decade included a 20 per cent share in the Morgan Guaranty and Trust Company and 5 per cent shares in the Bank of Tokyo, the Banque National de Paris, Deutsche Bank, National Westminster Bank and the Union Bank of Switzerland. Two Saudi commercial banks, the National Commerce Bank and the Bank of Riyadh, have also bought 5 per cent of the shares of these international banks. In addition, according to a Chase Manhatten study, direct deposits have been made at the multi-billion dollar level in US financial instruments and corporate shares. SAMA, for example, has reportedly invested $300 million in IBM stock, $250 million in the GM Acceptance Corp., $200 million in US Steel and $75 million in the Dallas Power and Light Co.[25] This short list does not accurately display the massive amount of debt obligations, mineral options, stocks and real estate that Saudi agencies own in Europe, Japan and the United States. In 1977 alone Saudis bought more than 83 tons of Swiss gold.[26]

The investment goals of SAMA and SIB changed somewhat with the writing of the third plan. Inflation in the West in 1979 and 1980 undermined the Saudi government's level of trust in the Western banking system and it decided to develop its own competitive banking system.[27] To this end the government asked its agencies to find optimal investments in companies active in export banking and other financial services that might include the transfer of technology back to the Kingdom.

MACROECONOMIC AGENDA

The overriding concerns in the third plan were controlling the import sector, and the country's ability to control inflation and deepen its absorptive capacity. The government's ability to control activities that increase inflation and import consumption and its thin absorptive capacity were complicated by the investment proposals set out in the second and third plans, many of which were fiscally debilitating. The expansionary policies followed by King Khalid's ministers in the mid-1970s had produced unexpected and very high rates of inflation. According to International Monetary Fund estimates, inflation reached 35.4 per cent in 1975 and 41.3 per cent in 1976.[28] This situation became a major concern when writing the third plan.

One of the main reasons for the country's inflation problem was its heavy dependence on foreign trade. The impact of increased import prices on domestic price levels had begun to be felt in the early 1970s. At that time most of Saudi Arabia's major trading partners had already begun to experience inflationary pressures in their own economies, and were still experiencing global inflationary problems.[29] Viewing the volume of imports from Western countries and considering the proportion of imports each year, a clear pattern between the world's inflation rates and Saudi Arabia's emerges. During the period 1979–80 a 1 per cent rise in the export prices of industrial countries resulted in a direct 0.5 per cent increase in Saudi Arabia's import prices. This came at the very time when the Saudi government had decided to accelerate its development construction schedules, causing domestic demand to rise at a much faster rate than the rate of growth of domestic production. Urbanisation reached phenomenal levels (see Mubarak, Chapter 4). This may all be seen as a reaction to extensive government spending, higher wages, increased personal spending per capita and, above all, a huge influx of foreign products into the Saudi marketplace.

The government's capital distribution through construction spending forced private consumers to increase their consumption of imported goods because the operational factories that had been constructed during the first plan period were already operating at capacity. Thus demand for imported goods increased and consumers were forced to compete directly with the government in a sellers' market. The lure of higher wages caused large-scale migration from the country side to the city, causing housing shortages and urban crowding. Civil servants, for example, enjoyed salary increases of over 100 per cent in the year following the oil embargo. This caused an unexpectedly rapid urbanisation movement that placed a great strain on the availability of food and other consumer products in the cities and left fewer persons to work on subsistence farms. In addition housing prices in Riyadh, Jeddah and Dammam rose dramatically.

The same inflationary process was also taking place in the business-to-business market. Domestic suppliers had long backlogs in their order books. New manufacturing firms began bidding wars against each other for labour and materials, and the bids placed by the government for materials and labour increasingly became the base at which private contractors were forced to compete. The results of this process were twofold. First, there was a large influx of foreign labour into the Kingdom's private sector, and even in to many government-financed projects. Second, spending money that had not been earned through profit-generated sales caused the monetary surplus to be absorbed through an increase in the level of prices. The purchase of foreign debt helped to relieve some of the inflationary pressure in 1977 and 1978, but by 1980 it had become clear that this approach would lead to increased government income via interest payments that could not be absorbed into the domestic economy.[30]

The third plan provided some economic setting and base for increased absorptive capacity by providing increased infrastructure, some new basic industries, some new consumer industries, new vocational and educational facilities, and incentives to develop small and medium-sized service businesses. Moreover the plan recognised that much of the country's absorptive-capacity problem would be resolved once the industrial facilities planned for completion over the next five years became operational. It assumed, with the help of short-term price subsidies, that completion of the above mentioned projects would lead to the absorptive capacity being considerably deepened by domestic production and the repatriation of much of the country's foreign labour force. Nonetheless, absorptive capacity limitations on the productivity of new investments were so acute during the second plan period that it limited the effectiveness of all new real investment, especially from the private sector.[31]

CONCLUSION

Against this background, Saudi Arabia's investment dilemmas at the time of the introduction of the third Five Year Development Plan became clearer. The Kingdom was still engaged in rapid industrialisation programmes costing billions of dollars that could otherwise have been invested abroad. Oil revenue surpluses for the Kingdom were projected to reach $130 billion in 1981. For most industrialised nations, how to invest these billions would not have been much of a problem. This was not the case with Saudi Arabia, and understanding its dilemmas requires an analysis of the various social, political and economic complexities that have been presented here in historical perspective.

It can be concluded, however, that the Saudi government approached the planning process in the second and third plans by recognising three factors. First, rapid industrial development and urbanisation would cause many social changes, and if these changes were to have a positive effect on the country the government would have to provide increased educational, health care, housing and social welfare services. The government has clearly done this part of the job, as by the end of the term of the third plan the Kingdom could boast some of the world's best hospitals, schools and research facilities. But the construction side of the social planning process was the easy part. Much more difficult was correctly predicting the impact of development on the political, social and religious mood of the people. This caused the plans' writers to include many short-term and stop-gap measures that would help people to deal with the hectic pace of modernisation.

Second, it was only in the two decades that spanned the second and third plans that a significant movement towards industrial development was achieved. The Kingdom needed to rid itself as much as possible of its dependency on foreign labour, products and political policies. It recognised that the quickest means of doing this was to limit foreign involvement in the industrial sector to a short period only, preferably less than 20 years, during which time its own people could be trained to take over the sectors dominated by foreign management and incentives to develop an indigenous entrepreneurial class could take effect. The planned move away from dependency on foreigners can be seen more clearly in the fourth and fifth development plans.

The third and final factor is the necessity to plan for the days when oil revenue can no longer sustain economic growth. This concern has necessitated the investment of billions of dollars in overseas assets. Their purpose is to provide a steady and consistent income to the government in periods when domestic income and international oil sales cannot meet the Kingdom's domestic requirements. Although the period of low oil prices in the 1980s was short term, it did serve to vindicate the Kingdom's decision to buy long-term financial investments abroad, which also financed the completion of construction projects in the mid-1980s and Saudi Arabia's involvement in Gulf War.

The effects of the oil crisis of the 1980s and the Gulf War in 1991 will be discussed in the next two chapters. The Kingdom's success in weathering these two storms was largely due to the planning efforts that took place from 1975 to 1980. It was in this period that the Kingdom made its most determined attempt to broaden the base of its economy. It was also during this period that the government began to take a global view of its economic system and to ensure that its domestic planning policies would put Saudi Arabia among the world's leading industrialised countries. These goals remain to be met, but its people and their businesses are clearly moving in that direction.

Notes and References

1. This chapter was written by J. W. Wright, Jr., based on Dr Ballool's PhD dissertion.
2. Saudi Arabian Monetary Agency (SAMA), Annual Report 1979 (Saudi Arabia: SAMA, 1979).
3. B. M. Hela, 'The Depletion of Exhaustible Resources: Some Theoretical Issues', in M. Parkin and R. Nobay, (eds), *Issues in Contemporary Economics* (Manchester: Manchester University Press, 1974), p. 211.
4. Ministry of Planning, *Second Development Plan: 1975–1980* (Riyadh: Ministry of Planning, 1975).
5. Kingdom of Saudi Arabia, *Wadi Jizan Land and Development Project* (Riyadh: Ministry of Agriculture and Water, 1959).
6. The United Nations, *Studies on Development Problems in Selected Countries of the Middle East* (New York: The United Nations, 1974), p.25.
7. Jean Paul Cleron, *Saudi Arabia 2000* (London: Croom Helm, 1978), p.49.
8. David Edans and William Snavely, 'Planning for Economic Development in Saudi Arabia', *Middle East Journal*, Winter 1970, p. 18.
9. Ministry of Planning, *Second Development Plan: 1975–1980* (Riyadh: Ministry of Planning, 1976), pp. 3–4.
10. *Second Development Plan*, op. cit., p. 5.
11. Ziauddin Sardarm, 'Saudis Warm to Solar Energy', *Nature*, 29 June 1978, pp. 700–1.
12. John Whelan, 'Ports' Chief Defies Shippers to Raise Unilaterally', *Middle East Economic Digest*, 25 August 1978, pp. 10–11.
13. Ramon Knauerhase, *The Saudi Arabian Economy* (New York: Praeger, 1975), p. 66. This figure was significantly lower then the 90 per cent of ten years earlier.
14. N. Fallen, *Middle East Oil Money and its Future Expenditure* (London: Graham & Trotman, 1975).
15. Saudi Arabian Monetary Agency, *Annual Report* (Riyadh: SAMA, 1979), p. 167.
16. Knauerhase, op. cit., p. 192.
17. Yusif A. Sayigh, *The Economics of the Arab World* (London: Croom Helm, 1978), p. 146.
18. *Arab Economic Report*, 1974, pp. 392–3.
19. Ministry of Planning, *Third Development Plan, 1980–1985* (Riyadh: Ministry of Planning, 1980).
20. The Industrial Studies and Development Center, *A Guide to Industrial Investment in Saudi Arabia*, 5th edn (Riyadh: The Industrial Studies and

Development Center, 1977), pp. 14–15. See also: City Bank, *Investment Guide to Saudi Arabia* (Riyadh: Citibank, 1975), p. 10.

21. Metra Consulting, *Saudi Arabia: Business Opportunities I and II* (London: Metra Consulting, 1975 and 1979).
22. *Third Development Plan*, op. cit.
23. Industrial Studies and Development Center, *Industrial Structure and Development in Saudi Arabia* (Riyadh: The Industrial Studies and Development Center, 1977), p. 17.
24. 'Saudi Arabia', *The Banker*, October 1980, p. 89.
25. The *Wall Street Journal*, 13 March 1981.
26. 'Gold Shipped to the Middle East', *The Banker*, October 1980, pp. 15–16. In reality this figure grossly underrepresents the level of gold traded in Gulf countries. For example, in 1996 a single transaction between a Qatari seller and an Emirate buyer transferred 78 ton of gold bullion. While transactions such as these can be verifies, estimates of total bullion holdings are difficult to make. It is likely that Gulf Arabs own hundreds of thousands of tons of gold.
27. *The Economist*, '*International Banking: Survey*', 22 March 1980, p. 20.
28. International Monetary Fund, *International Financial Statistics*, vol. XXIXX, no. 9 (Washington, DC: International Monetary Fund, September 1976).
29. *The Economist*, 1 December 1979, p. 70.
30. Economist use 'absorptive capacity' in a variety of ways and it is helpful to differentiate between capital-absorptive capacity and expenditure-absorptive capacity. I will consider only the concept of capital-absorptive capacity, which is defined for an oil-based economy in John H. Adler, *Absorptive Capacity: The Concept and Its Determinations* (Washington, DC: The Brookings Institution, 1975).
31. R. S. Eckans, 'Absorptive Capacity as a Constraint Due to Maturation Processes', in J. Bhagwati and R. S. Eckans (eds), *Development and Planning* (Cambridge, MA: MIT Press, 1972), pp. 79–108.

3 Private Sector Finance: Problems Faced by the Fourth and Fifth Five Year Development Plans

J. W. Wright, Jr with Abdullah H. Albatel[1]

This chapter deals with changes in emphasis towards 'real' sector productivity in the private sector of the economy while the Saudi government was planning for the 1985–95 period. It surveys both the growth and development of the private sector and the roles the government wishes that sector to play in the economy. It also touches on the roles the Kingdom's financial institutions are expected to play in implementing the fourth and fifth Five Year Development Plans.

Defining the 'real' or the 'producing' sector is more difficult in the Saudi Arabian economy than it is elsewhere. In 1979 Rodney Wilson wrote:

> In the Saudi Arabian case not only do oil and refined products move through trade, but also the labor and capital engaged in petroleum production. Wages and profits do not accrue for the most part to factors supplied by Saudi Arabia, and the country receives instead the residual income element as its main gain from trade.... The country has lacked both resources and the means to absorb this rentier income, or to use it to increase real wealth through the development of the domestic economy.[2]

Wilson's account was basically right for that period of time, as from 1973–83 the country was enjoying the benefits of the high revenues from oil. At that time more attention was given to investment in infrastructure development than to anything else. Since then the situation has changed significantly, and it has been recognised that diversification is needed to stimulate the economy and reduce the uncertainty of future income. In the development plans set out for 1985 and 1990 more attention was given to the private sector, particularly privately funded investment. The most direct reason for this diversification is the fact oil reserves will eventually be depleted, necessitating an alternative economic base of production.

Until recently investment has concentrated on infrastructure, petroleum light manufacturing, and construction materials. Most of the major projects in transportation, communications, health, education, electricity and water that were initiated in the 1970s were either completed during the term of the third plan or were due to be completed during the course of the fourth plan. Attention centred on industrial development in the mid-1970s to the mid-1980s, particularly in downstream activities of the petroleum sector and import substitution. Joint ventures with foreign partners were formed to utilise oil and gas feed stock for petroleum refining operations.[3] Diversification away from oil was needed to reduce the risk associated with dependency on one export commodity, hopefully benefiting the planning process and spurring long-term economic development and growth.[4] It was also felt, then as now, that an industrial base that flourished without the assistance of foreign expertise would reduce the external political–economic threats faced by the Kingdom.[5]

The fourth plan, covering the period 1985–90, had three main strategic economic goals, with some variations in emphasis over the first three plans:

1. The completion of infrastructure projects that had been set forth in the first three plans and, more importantly, the completion of the industrial estates at Yanbu and Jubail.
2. The expansion of social service programmes, particularly in the areas of education on a broad level, and management and vocational training in more specific terms. Hospitals and health centres also received high priority.
3. The promotion of economic growth through encouragement of the private sector. The public sector, it was decided, should push the private sector towards economic activities that are removed from the production and exportation of crude oil.

The fourth plan set total government spending at about $278 billion for the period 1986–90. Approximately 50 per cent of this expenditure was allocated to development programmes that would increase the operational efficiency of oil facilities (training in high-technology petrochemical production), provide productivity incentives in agriculture, finance and manufacturing, reduce the number of unskilled foreign workers and promote entrepreneurship and small business activities. The plan envisaged a much more active role by the private sector in industries currently financed or administered by the government. It also encouraged private sector investment in the country.

The plan met with relative success over the five-year period it covered. In 1989 the share of oil and gas in GDP declined to about half its 1970s level, while most other sectors increased their share. This indicated a maturing of the economy as a result of greater diversification. The plan's success in this area was tempered, however, by the oil-price and production cutbacks in the 1980s. A negative effect of the plan was seen in the construction sector, which reached its peak in 1982–83. This sector's sharp decline during the fourth plan years was predictable because of the completion of major infrastructure projects and the decrease in revenues that were earmarked for new real estate projects. The government sector, which had expanded twice during the 1970–85 period, remained constant between 1985 and 1990.

The trade sector showed impressive movement. In terms of relative shares per sector, by nominal value, enterprises producing real goods showed the highest rates of growth in the economy (Tables 3.1 and 3.2).

This movement away from nominal shares towards real value shares can be explained by the higher than average gains in prices for real goods as opposed to oil or compared with the lower than average price rises in services. Accordingly, the highest rates of growth were found in agriculture (8.8 per cent), manufacturing (4.0 per cent), government services (2.7 per cent) and financial services (2.1 per cent). Ten years earlier construction had been by far the fastest growing real producer (58.3 per cent).

During the fourth plan years SABIC (the Saudi Arabian Basic Industries Corporation) made moves to fund high-technology

Table 3.1 Annual percentage growth rate of real output by sector

	1975–80	*1980–85*
Producing sector:		
Agriculture	5.1	6.2
Mining	4.6	−16.5
Manufacturing	9.8	6.9
Utilities	21.9	18.6
Construction	15.8	−0.9
Sub total	6.9	−7.2
Service sector:		
Trade	22.7	9.2
Transport	19.3	7.1
Finance	14.0	4.4
Other services	3.3	1.9
Government	–	6.4
Sub total	15.1	6.9
Total non oil sector	14.8	6.4
Oil sector	4.8	−14.2

downstream manufacturing projects. SABIC was changed with three tasks. First, it was to implement plans to expand production in petrochemicals, fertilisers and other hydrocarbon industries. The high-technology hydrocarbon industries were 'expected to be a training ground for the Saudi work force and to spur growth in other industries'.[6] Second, SABIC was to fund more private sector activities in the aluminum, iron and steel industries. Finally, it was asked to sell up to 75 per cent of its shares to the public over the course of the plan. By 1988 it was estimated that Saudi Arabian petrochemical output accounted for 5 per cent of world production, up from less than 1 per cent ten years earlier.[7]

The importance of the private sector's role in the economy and in the broader development of the country was a consistent feature in the fourth and fifth plans, although the complete transition from a construction-oriented, government-financed oriented economic structure was not as notable in the fourth plan as it is in the fifth. In the fourth plan four semi-government companies are appointed to assist in the privatisation of the Saudi economy: the National Industrialization Company (NIC), the Saudi

Table 3.2 Sectoral percentage share of gross domestic product (per cent)

	1973	*1975*	*1980*	*1985*	*1990*
Producing sectors:					
Agriculture	1.0	0.9	5.4	4.1	4.8
Mining	0.2	0.4	1.0	1.1	1.1
Manufacturing	1.4	1.9	4.8	7.3	10.4
Petrochemicals	–	–	–	–	2.6
Utilities	–	0.1	0.2	0.5	0.5
Construction	8.4	12.9	32.3	23.5	17.7
Sub total	11.0	16.2	41.8	36.5	37.1
Service sector:					
Trade	2.7	4.9	13.2	15.8	15.5
Transport	3.2	5.6	11.8	13.0	14.3
Real estate	–	–	8.0	7.1	6.2
Finance	2.9	3.7	3.4	5.0	6.6
Other services	1.1	1.5	3.9	4.5	4.6
Government	6.5	5.9	17.5	18.1	15.7
Sub total	16.4	21.6	58.2	63.5	62.9
Total non oil sector	27.4	37.8	34.8	60.2	57.1
Oil sector	72.6	62.2	65.2	39.8	42.9
Total	100.0	100.0	100.0	100.0	100.0

Advanced Industries Fund (SAIC), the Saudi Venture Capital Fund (SVCG) and the Saudi Industrial Development Fund (SDIC). However, the language used to outline their functions is vague. In contrast to weak verbiage calling for more participation, the language used in the fifth plan is much more specific – that the private sector should become the 'driving force' of the economy in 'manufacturing, finance, construction, and agriculture', and it vows to 'facilitate a stronger and more diversified private sector [by creating] a positive environment for the private sector [to] establish new institutions [and to] invest in, develop and manage profitable enterprises'.[8] (5th Dev. Plan citation is correct).

The importance of the manufacturing sector stems from its potential role in achieving diversification. Relying on one source or sector for revenue would put the country in a risky position in times of adverse economic shocks. The government is therefore endeavoring to help the manufacturing sector by providing indirect subsidies such as low utility rates, modern industrial zones and research assistance. A more direct benefit to the private sector was provided by agencies such as the Private Investment Fund and the Saudi Industrial Development Fund (SIDF), which spent a combined $3.3 billion in the 1970s. Azzam estimates that the various government development agencies provided close to $60 billion in interest-free loans between 1970 and 1985.[9]

These development finance agencies remained the main funding sources for the construction of manufacturing facilities during the fourth and fifth plan years. However programmes were mounted that redefined the level of participation that was encouraged/expected from private sector business owners in both plans, but more so in the fifth plan. As a result the level of private sector investment vis-à-vis public sector investment rose from 27.4 per cent in 1980 to 50.2 per cent in 1989.[10] Private expenditure rose from $10.5 billion during the third plan to $11.65 billion (constant dollars) during the fourth plan. In a period marked by decreasing government revenues, this represented a major restructuring of the Kingdom's investment structure toward' private sector funding, and this is expected to continue into the 1990s.

The fifth plan indicates that many studies and surveys show that the private sector has developed rapidly and now enjoys several strengths and advantageous conditions that are enhancing private investment activity. However, several constraints now faced the private sector, including (1) its historical dependence on government expenditure, particularly on the part of contracting companies, which is affecting its ability to diversify into production activities that are independent of government expenditure; (2) underutilisation of existing capacity because of the small domestic market and problems related to the development of non-oil exports; and (3) high average production costs and the lack of internal and external economies of large-scale production, in addition to marketing problems, particularly in agriculture.

Even though the government is attempting to delegate most of the responsibility to the private sector in the fifth plan, it is not willing to pull out of the development process altogether, and it probably should not. The fifth plan calls on the government to continue to aid the private sector in many ways. It will make available long-term loans at low or zero interest rates, make it possible to protect new industries through the provision of low-charge feasibility studies, and provide a wide range of incentives for participating in the production process. It will participate in the production process itself where necessary to awaken the private sector to the possibilities of long-term gains through capital formation. Government investment is planned to help to break down some of the discontinuities inherent in the earlier phases of the country's development. Most importantly, it will try to help industry to provide training and development programmes that will create economies of scale in many areas.[11]

Policies for financial-system development merge in the fourth and fifth plans. The rapid decline in government revenues caused by the fall in oil prices sent shockwaves through the Saudi banking system in 1986–88, although the pressure was already being felt when the fourth plan was being drafted. But while national revenues had fallen dramatically, the fourth plan clearly called for expansion of the financial sector. The mandate includes promoting the incorporation of national financial institutions for the investment of private funds within the country; urging commercial banks to extend their credit facilities to production projects instead of concentrating on import trade; encouraging the incorporation of more joint-stock companies to undertake large projects with economies of scale, so that the greatest number of citizens may benefit from investment opportunities; creating a system, under government supervision, for the exchange of company shares, with the objective of encouraging investment and avoiding the pitfalls of financial speculation (which is against Islamic law); encouraging the public to invest in worthwhile industries using few raw material and production methods that require minimum labour and minimum quantities of critical physical resources such as water; encouraging the public to invest in agriculture by establishing joint-stock companies to undertake large agricultural projects using modern farm equipment and irrigation techniques; encouraging a more rational preinvestment evaluation of projects; and promoting the adoption of new technologies.

The fifth plan continues along this line and stresses the need for an advanced financial system:

> Although the financial system in the Kingdom has developed dramatically during the last two decades, it needs further strengthening in each of these dimensions to meet the investment requirements of the fifth plan more effectively. In this regard, there is a need to expand the range of investment alternatives for savers and asset holders. Opportunities for individuals to invest their personal savings in productive enterprises in the Kingdom rather than in the international money markets or in physical assets, such as land and gold, need to be developed. An important step in this direction was taken in the last two years of the fourth plan with the issuance of government development bonds, thereby promoting both savings and opportunities for individual investors to increase their participation in the development process. The development of long-term debt instruments and equity markets will create more investment opportunities and will add to the development of a domestic capital market. Thus, a need arises for a growing share of the banking system's financial assets to be invested in the Kingdom, and for the range of financial services supporting the business sector to be expanded.[12]

According to the fifth plan, to achieve this ambitious investment target the following initiatives will be pursued: attracting a higher proportion of private savings for investment in the domestic economy by providing profitable, safe and marketable financial investments; encouraging banks to expand their domestic lending and provide a wide range of financial services; developing a more broadly based private financial system, through the growth of non-bank financial intermediaries whose services both compete with and complement the commercial banks, especially those which are potential sources of long-term credit, such as equipment leasing companies and cooperative insurance companies; and encouraging the development of efficient capital markets, particularly a more active and efficient equity market.

The plan also indicates that the financial system needs to be more efficient in supporting export trade and calls for a feasibility study to establish a specialised institution to promote Saudi exports. This proposed institution will seek to provide commercial loans to finance local working capital and export operations. Currently this type of service is not provided by the commercial banks, which usually confine their financing activities to the transfer of payment when delivery actually takes place.

An export development bank would offer exporters two main services. The first relates to working capital loans to be made available to Saudi exporters by commercial banks before actual export delivery took place. The export bank would guarantee repayment of, for example, 80 per cent of the principle, so the commercial banks would bear only a 20 per cent risk on the loan. Second, credit insurance would be sold to cover in full export losses resulting from war, expropriation and currency inconvertibility, and to partially cover commercial losses arising from nonpayment by the buyer as a result of insolvency or default.

Specific figures are also given in the fifth plan for the further development of a more effective stock exchange. The Saudi Arabian corporate securities market has expanded significantly in recent years, the value of shares traded through the commercial banks having risen to SR 1.9 billion in 1988.

The government feels that a properly regulated and active stock exchange could play a critical part in the economy's development through stimulating the supply of capital stock to business enterprises; creating opportunities for the public to participate in the ownership of companies, leading to a more broadly based contribution in support of private sector development; encouraging greater use of financial vehicles whereby an adequate range of risk/profit opportunities is made available to private investors; helping to expand domestic savings and investment; and establishing fair prices and practices for securities and minimum cost trading, thus leading to a more efficient distribution of capital. The fifth plan also recognises that the current stock exchange mechanism is rather slow and very complicated, as the processing of a stock issue can take up to two years. Individual stock transactions require between one week and two months to complete, and more often than not buyers must reach sellers by their own means. Thus blocks of shares may not be broken up to match the needs of buyers. These obstacles result in significant gaps between bid and asking prices, thus indicating that the price mechanism is not working effectively. Therefore consideration will be given to the establishment of a more efficient stock exchange, with appropriate state regulation and control to avoid detrimental speculation. Given the rapid technological improvements in computer-based stock transactions, there is an excellent opportunity to introduce state-of-the-art systems that would be compatible with other GCC stock exchanges.

Other types of financial development proposed in the fifth plan encourage the establishment of leasing companies, an increase in the number of insurance companies and enhanced power among equity lending companies. These ventures are expected to complement the improvements that were developed during the fourth plan years. Commercial banks are increasing their investment in and credit to domestic borrowers and investors. Deposits, loans and number of bank branches have all increased, as shown in Table 3.3, and since 1987 nearly 100 development

Table 3.3 Saudi Arabian commercial bank portfolio distributions as of 1989 ($ million)

Bank	*Total assets*	*Loans*	*Equity*	*Profit (loss)*
National Commercial Bank	23 100.8	9940.0	853.3	0.0
Riyadh Bank	11 322.8	2705.9	1120.0	67.9
Saudi American Bank	7 078.6	1757.8	514.6	112.5
al-Bank al-Saudi al-Fransi	4 807.2	1381.5	293.9	27.5
al-Rajhi Banking and Investment Corportion	4 470.7	N/A	561.1	274.1
Arab National Bank	4 187.2	982.3	496.4	86.0
Saudi British Bank	3 351.0	732.0	191.2	32.9
al-Bank al-Saudi al-Hollandi	2 732.7	730.8	178.0	21.3
Saudi Cairo Bank	N/A	N/A	N/A	N/A
United Saudi Commercial Bank	1 377.8	258.7	85.4	25.5
Saudi Investment Bank	1 337.5	165.8	59.0	2.9
Bank al-Jazira	1 292.1	488.9	62.6	(19.8)

Sources: Compiled from *MEED*, August 1990, (34): 13; *MEED*, June 1989, (35): 5.

bond issues available in denominations of SR 50 000, 100 000, 500 000 and 1 000 000 with maturity ranging from two to five years, have been offered on the market.[13]

The Kingdom's budget has several unique features that make controlling financial reserves and the money supply difficult. In theory, revenues in excess of spending should not be a problem. The excess revenue could be invested in low-risk, interest-bearing foreign assets. The decision as to how much oil to produce and how much excess revenue to acquire should depend on whether the interest on foreign assets gives a better or worse rate of return than keeping the oil in the ground.

In practice, however, in Saudi Arabia the production of excess revenue creates major problems. All oil revenues accrue directly to the government and the only way that individual citizens can benefit is through the government's spending decisions. When the budget is in substantial surplus there is a strong short-term incentive to increase spending. Moreover real income is dependent upon the ability to import goods and services, rather than on the ability to produce goods and services. By the same token government spending on stimulative policies directly increases the money supply because of the underdeveloped state of Saudi financial markets.

In fact, according to SAMA reports the currency ratio has declined steadily over the past ten years or so (Table 3.4), reflecting the incentive the public has to hold an increasing share of its wealth in deposit form rather than in currency.[14] This is a symptom of the financial deepening that has taken place in the broad economic system. In 1989 the share of M1 in M3 declined from 80.4 per cent to 50.9 per cent, and the shares of quasi-money increased from 19.6 per cent in 1965 to 49.1 per cent in 1989.

Table 3.4 Money supply ratios

	1965	*1970*	*1975*	*1980*	*1985*	*1989*
Currency ratio	2.085	2.034	0.905	0.773	0.757	0.585
Currency share in M3	0.543	0.493	0.373	0.308	0.242	0.188
M1 and M3	0.804	0.736	0.784	0.706	0.571	0.509
M3 quasi money share	0.196	0.265	0.216	0.294	0.438	0.491

However, total money supply is simultaneously determined by the behaviour of the Central Bank, in this case SAMA, the commercial banks and the public. The central bank's behaviour is summarised by movements in reserve money, and the behaviour of the banks is characterised by movements in the money multiplier. In Saudi Arabia the dominant element behind the growth in monetary aggregates is SAMA's reserve money – not the savings of businesses or individuals, whose effect on the financial system pales in comparison with the money pools controlled by SAMA. SAMA's control of reserves is directly proportional to its ability to control the size of its balance sheet.[15]

The two dominant elements in SAMA's balance sheet are foreign assets and government deposits. Because Saudi banks always invest their deposits outside the country, where they can earn market interest rates,[16] foreign assets add to reserve money while government deposits reduce these reserves. When they increase together, as they typically do, there will be no change in reserve money. In essence the major obstacle to SAMA's ability to control the money supply is the size and composition of its own reserves. This is a clear case where fiscal and monetary policy are not separate but rather a single tool. In this regard, unique to the Gulf Arab states and possibly one or two other OPEC members, fiscal decisions determine the growth of money supply in Saudi Arabia.

There is also a very close link between the growth of foreign assets and the growth of government deposits, where leakages in deposits in foreign assets act as an automatic stabiliser on the growth of reserve money. In effect the difference between foreign assets and government deposits determines reserve money. Therefore, over time reserve money is changed when foreign assets induce parallel changes in government deposits. Knowing that foreign assets almost always increase in Saudi's case at a somewhat faster rate than government deposits, and that when a substantial acceleration in foreign assets is associated with a slowdown in government deposit growth, we know that reserve money tends to accelerate about one year after a sharp acceleration in foreign asset investment.

This automatic process can be described as an initial injection of reserve money and is offset by a series of leakages. These potential leakages are associated with government purchases of foreign goods and services, private sector purchases of foreign assets and/or purchases of domestic financial assets other than currency. Therefore, if the fifth plan succeeds in inducing domestic reinvestment it will reduce the private sector's dependence on government-sponsored funding, but it will also fill a major leak in the automatic money supply control system, which is itself dependent on private sector investment in foreign assets. This will exacerbate SAMA's planning problems in the face of monetary surpluses when they occur, while at the same time private sector reinvestment should raise the relative rate of government deposit activity, complicating SAMA's situation in the face of a fiscal policy forced into retrenchment by policies meant to control inflation.

Saudi Arabia's budget planning system is also complicated by the very notion and definition of a balanced budget. In spite of a substantial budget surplus, the Kingdom has experienced a large increase in currency issues from the central bank. This is contrary to what would be expected to occur with large and persistent surpluses such as those seen prior to 1982. The reason for this is that during the first three plans Saudi Arabia ran its budget in only a narrow accounting sense and not in a real economic sense. An 'economic' balanced budget is one where the demand for resources (spending) is equal to a government-induced reduction in the demand for resources by the private sector (receipts).

In Saudi Arabia, accounting and economic balanced budgets are different because a large proportion of government revenue is extracted from non-resident foreigners as oil royalties rather than coming from domestic taxes. In this special case, economic balance is equality between government spending and imports of foreign goods, services and financial assets. Government spending in excess of these imports would represent a net fiscal stimulation of the private economy, and therefore would be exactly anomalous to a budget deficit in most other countries. This economic deficit is financed in Saudi Arabia by central bank monetisation, which leads to a rise in reserve money and currency, which in turn contributes to inflation.

There are only three effective means that central banks typically have to encourage money supply restraint in the face of current conditions. Until recently SAMA has had only one of three traditional tools for effecting monetary policy. Open-market operations were excluded as a potential tool, partly because the large cumulative government balances made it unnecessary to issue debt until the term of the fourth plan, and partly because the legal prohibition on interest payments prevented the development of a domestic debt securities market. The discount rate is not a viable tool either, because SAMA's charter does not allow it to lend to commercial banks or to receive interest, leaving reserve requirements as its primary monetary tool.

Hence we see another paradox in Saudi Arabia's money supply cycle. To date the private sector has not been effective in creating profit-side retained earnings, nor has it generated a substantial repatriation of money through the sale of non-oil exports. SAMA's reluctance to pursue an active policy of monetary control via the reserve requirement reflects the fact that most domestic money creation results from government spending on loan programmes, rather than from lending and investment activities by commercial banks. If most domestic liquidity is created outside commercial banks, any action by SAMA to restrain their activities would contribute to the relative decline of those institutions to service and promote the private sector. In addition, if bank loans are an important source of private sector reinvestment, then squeezing the banks would reduce the production capacity of the economy, defeating the central theme of the fourth and especially the fifth plans: entrepreneurial development.

In recognition of this unusual system of capital flow, the fifth plan treats commercial banks as the most important intermediary link to small and medium-sized businesses in the private sector. Currently Saudi commercial banks provide mainly short-term credit to the private sector, one third of which goes to quick-turnover trade finance, where debts are repaid when the products are sold. These loans are primarily issued to finance import trading. Prior to 1985, when only 10 per cent of loans were made to finance private sector working capital, commercial banks tended to ignore private sector and consumer credit markets. Instead they usually participated in loans where the majority financier was the government or a government-sponsored agency.

In response to the commercial banks' ignorance of the local commercial market, lending in the SR 5 billion market became dominated by individuals or small groups who were willing to finance cars and consumer durables. Loans for agriculture have represented less than 1 per cent of total commercial bank credit.

As stated earlier, the fourth plan intended bank credit to be provided in larger amounts to the rapidly developing private manufacturing sector. Unfortunately this did not happen. The manufacturing sector increased its share of bank loans from 5.9 per cent in 1970 to 15.3 per cent in 1975, but its credit share stayed at around 9–10 per cent for the years 1975–85 and then dropped to 6 per cent in 1989. The problem is that private sector development requires non-government-sponsored and non-infrastructure construction, which the commercial banks deem to be risky ventures and are therefore 'cautious of too heavy involvement'.[17] Trade finance also fell during the term of the fourth plan, from 36.2 per cent of total commercial credit in 1985 to 26.3 per cent in 1989. The winners in terms of credit extension between 1985 and 1989 were finance (2.8 per cent to 12.5 per cent) and the 'other' category (13.7 per cent to 22.6 per cent), predominantly leasing, consumer and export credit.

The need to control the money supply and encourage local reinvestment is what led SAMA to issue the development bonds discussed earlier. It is also the reason the country is trying to develop a functional stock market system. The current stock market is relatively new and only open to Saudi citizens trading in the shares of privatised companies.

Currently 52 companies are traded on the Saudi stock exchange. These companies fall into four categories: financial, industrial, utilities and agriculture. The number of transactions rose from 7842 in 1985 to 110 030 in 1989, and the value of the shares traded rose from SR 760 million to nearly SR 3.4 billion over the same period. While this progress is impressive, the Saudi stock market is far from being a mature market that is able to help small and medium-sized businesses find the capital they need. Banks often choose to match buyers and sellers internally rather than utilise the central exchange. This situation causes low volume and lack of coordination between banks and renders the monetary system unable to provide liquidity to the market.

This institutional structure provides banks with little incentives to find the best price for their customers. The fifth plan does little more than make overtures towards the development of the stock market as a viable vehicle for raising capital for corporations. The plan's failure to address the real problems that face the Saudi stock market confirms its belief that the most important intermediaries between the oil-rich government and the private sector is the commercial banking system.

It is impossible to know at this point if the directives in the fifth plan concerning increased commercial bank activity will be carried out. The plan does, however, clearly criticise the financial system for its inadequacy with regard to the number of non-agency financial institutions, the lack of control of the unofficial money-lending market, and lack of control by SAMA of the composition of bank assets. More importantly, the plan shows an intention for much of the financing of private activity that has been assumed by the government-subsidised specialised banks to be transferred to commercial banks. Given the inability or unwillingness of the government to maintain the level of subsidies to the private sector, their main source of available capital over the next few years will be commercial banks, but only if the banks divert assets from foreign investment to domestic lending.

This will be a very complicated process to implement and manage. As Looney puts it, 'The current danger [as seen in the fifth plan] is that banks and private sector alike will react in the opposite direction by failing to provide an adequate level of financing, as a consequence of the short-term signals currently affecting decision-making in the Kingdom'.[18] It is clear that the government has the ability to play an active role in stabilising the level of the deposits in the financial system. But it is also quite possible, as we saw in the mid-1980s, that the withdrawal of funds could cause severe liquidity problems. In addition, with out government-backed reinsurance will commercial banks be willing to issue risky loans to the developing private sector?

Still, it must be concluded that the non-oil private sector has grown at a healthy rate, reflecting a degree of institutional migration. One indicator is the rise in the number of industrial licences awarded by the Ministry of Industry and Electricity: from 492 in

1975 to 2114 in 1981 and 7107 in 1989. During the same period the number of operating factories in the country increased from 479 in 1975 to 1219 in 1981 and 2251 in 1989.[19]

The fifth plan shows a definite intention, as did the fourth plan, to facilitate the growth of the private sector. The obstacles to doing so are many and are unaccounted for in traditional theories of economic development planning. However, despite the dominance of the government in the economic performance of the Saudi Arabian economy, the non-oil private sector's spending on capital formation has increased by 24.6 per cent per annum. The government's policy is to encourage the private sector to take an active part in the country's investment. Now the challenge lies with the private sector, including privately held commercial banks, which need to invest in new industries. At the heart of the fifth plan is an expectation that the private sector will take responsibility for future economic growth. But it clearly shows that this responsibility is to be shared by the Kingdom's commercial banks and financial institutions.

Notes and References

1. Dr Albatel has recently defended his dissertation on 'The Roles of Financial Institutions in Economic Development: Savings, Investment and Income Growth – The Case of Saudi Arabia', thereby completings his PhD in Economics from Northern Illinois University, Delkalb, Illinois. This essay was edited by J. W. Wright, Jr, with permission, based on Chapter 3 of Dr Albatel's dissertation. Publication here does not restrict Dr Albatel's use of this information in other publications.
2. Rodney Wilson, *The Economies of the Middle East* (London: Macmillan, 1979), pp. 40, 44.
3. D. Wells, 'The Effects of Saudi Industrialization on Employment', *Journal of Energy and Development*, vol. 11, no. 2 (1986), pp. 273–84.
4. H. Askari, *Saudi Arabian Economy: Oil and the Search for Economic Development* (London: AJI Press, 1990), p. 23.
5. J. Presley, *A Guide to the Saudi Arabian Economy* (New York: St. Martin's Press, 1984), p. 49.
6. A. Al-Johany, M. Berne and J. W. Mixon, Jr, *The Saudi Arabian Economy* (Baltimore, MD: The John Hopkins University Press, 1986), p. 121.
7. R. E. Looney, 'The Impact of Technology Transfer on the Structure of the Saudi Arabian Labor Force', *Journal of Economic Issues*, vol. 22, no. 2 (1988), pp. 485–92.
8. Government of Saudi Arabia Ministry of Planning, *Fifth Development Planning* (Riyadh, 1990), pp. 139–40.

9. H. Azzam, *The Gulf Economies in Transition* (London: Macmillan, 1988).
10. R. E. Looney, *Economic Development in Saudi Arabia: Consequences of the Oil Price Decline* (London: JAI Press, 1990), p. 163.
11. Wells, op. cit., p. 273.
12. Fifth Development Plan, op. cit., p. 155.
13. Saudi Arabian Monetary Agency (SAMA), *1989 Annual Report* (Riyadh: SAMA).
14. Saudi Arabia Monetary Agenciy, *Annual Reports and Statistical Summaries*, various issues (Riyadh: SAMA, 1965–89).
15. M. W. Keran, and A. A. Almalik, 'Monetary Sources of Inflation in Saudi Arabia', *Federal Reserve Bank–San Fransisco Economic Review Suppliment*, Winter 1979, pp. 5–27.
16. Economist Intelligence Unit, *Country Reports, Saudi Arabia*, no. 2 (1989), p. 26.
17. Looney, (1990) op. cit., p. 118.
18. Looney, (1990) op. cit., p. 122.
19. Saudi Arabian Ministry of Planning, *Facts and Figures* (Riyadh, 1990).

4 Cultural Continuity and Saudi Urban Planning: National, Regional and Municipal

J. Wright, Jr with Faisal A. Mubarak[1]

In other writings Mubarak's work has focused on the sociopolitical and economic processes of formation, growth and location that have primarily determined the shift, organisation and distribution of the contemporary spatial network in Saudi Arabia. The operation of these forces has been largely affected by the oil economy and political circumstances of the nation-state, but the scale of urbanisation must not be underestimated. The pace of urbanisation in the Arab Gulf states, with urban populations reaching 96 per cent, has not been matched by any other region of the world.[2] The restructuring of the national economy under the aegis of the new nation-state spurred the urbanisation process, and Saudi towns and settlements became loci of unprecedented growth, exhibiting overcrowding, high levels of chronic deprivation and poverty. In general the internal organisation of urban forms has remained free of public accountability and has taken place in an uncontrolled fashion.

During the early decades of the Kingdom (1930–60), new neighbourhoods sprouted that housed waves of 'urban villagers' in substandard residential stock, while Bedouins pitched their tents and constructed makeshift dwellings in undeveloped sections of towns or on their peripheries, forming *hilal*, communities of relatively homogeneous inhabitants sharing a tribal lineage or place of origin.[3] Under these circumstances, the government introduced a series of measures to circumscribe urban development and direct it toward socially desirable goals. These measures were *ad hoc* and were applied with few social and environmental considerations. Later these efforts developed into what is currently referred to as urban and regional planning in Saudi Arabia.

Overwhelmed by rapid change, local authorities in many Arab countries relied on Western models to assuage the negative outcomes that accompany rapid urbanisation. Western planning consultants were hired to draft comprehensive master plans. For example an American consulting firm was hired by the Libyan government to complete, in a period of a little less than two years, 35 long-term master plans for towns and cities.[4] Western paradigms have also come into vogue in Saudi Arabia through the training of Saudi architects and planners in Western institutions. The unguarded use of imported architecture and urban planning presents a paradox. As Stefano Bianca has written:

> Muslim societies are facing an ambiguous situation: in most countries, Islam still provides firm religious bonds and a strong sense of community. On the other hand, western institutions, political, economic and educational systems have been adopted, which to some extent contradict the Islamic way of life.... The tools of European civilization imply a value system and an ideology of their own, which is inseparable from the corresponding techniques.... Therefore, an indiscriminate use of these tools in the Islamic context will necessarily mean a cultural struggle and penetration by alien ideological concepts.[5]

In Saudi Arabia, more than in most Arab countries, there is deep concern about the maintenance of traditional values and bringing an indigenous identity to the contemporary environment. But due to rapid development there has been little time to ponder (or pander to) over culturally based design models and policies. The Western models employed in Saudi Arabia have not passed through critical assessment; they have been maintained essentially in their original forms.[6] It is interesting to note that urban planning efforts in Christian, Judaic and Muslim countries have been at odds for centuries. In Europe, Galantay wrote, 'Christianity strove to enhance its identity with respect to Judaism and to Islam, and fell back on classical traditions by embracing ... geometrical regularity in town planning and architecture'. Thus the orthogonal grid became associated with a sense of twelfth and thirteenth century Christian prosperity while the 'Islamic labyrinth' was linked by European theologians to evil. Even now Westerners see the Islamic style as 'an obstacle to modernization'.[7]

Today the contrasts seen in urban planning models are more politico-economic than religious. In Arab countries, rapid transformation occurred in dismal political and economic environments. The transition from traditional, preindustrial social systems to modern urban conglomerations was initiated by colonialism and later augmented by the subordination of the internal economies of the newly formed nation-states to the world's political–economic system. The presence of foreign powers in the path of cultural development precluded the development of local processes compatible with and geared to the local culture's needs. The departure of these colonial systems left behind a political vacuum that was filled by despotic military regimes and traditional monarchies. In the wake of Western technology, traditional urban design and building processes were rendered obsolete, less capable of meeting growth demand under rapid urbanisation. The substitution of the traditional ways of life and building techniques necessitated new concepts of spatial organisation, at the individual building level as well as on the city scale. Imported planning paradigms and construction methods, coupled with the introduction of the automobile, aborted old models and preempted indigenous development. Overwhelmed by rapid urbanisation, the fledgling states took on the task of urban planning. Urban planning has become the prerogative of the state, and it has therefore become an activity that has since remained concealed from the public.

To a very large extent, the colonisation of Arab territories by European powers forged the planning map. By the time of their departure these territories had been transformed into distinctive geographic entities with economies established during colonisation. New nation-states emerged, supplanting colonial control and predominantly governed by autocratic political systems. The newly established nation-states inherited a centralised framework of administration, which many specialists feel has generally restricted development'.

In Saudi Arabia, 'most of the members of the municipality are appointed'.[8] The main reason for this centrality is the rapidity of nomadic migration to the cities. Faced with a phenomenol rate of urbanisation that ran from 10–12 per cent per annum during the booming decade of the 1970s, the Saudi government has resorted to various forms of planning practices to assuage urbanisation's negative by-products – overcrowding, substandard housing, and a lack of sewage systems and public and social services. Between 1950 and 1985 the level of urbanisation in Saudi Arabia increased from 10 per cent to 75 per cent.[9] For example Dammam, the centre of oil industry activity in the Eastern Province, was transformed from a sleepy settlement of 300 huts in the 1930s to a teeming city of 450 000 people in 1986. Ninety per cent of Dammam's housing stock has been built during the last twenty years and 35 per cent in the last five years. Riyadh, the capital of the country, changed from a burgh of 19 000 inhabitants in the 1920s to a bustling metropolis of an estimated 1.3 million people in the mid-1980s. The discovery of oil in 1938 became the catalyst for an unprecedented urbanisation process. The oil income available to the central government was used to modernise the traditional society. Later, during the reign of King Faisal, rising oil revenues became large enough for the government to shift the economy into a higher gear that ultimately expedited the transformation of the physical environment.

A brief discussion of the development of government national planning apparatus and policy formulation in the Kingdom is needed to elucidate the direct role of the government in shaping the contemporary built environment. I will review the planning system, its components and processes, how urban planning evolved in the public sector, how it fits into the bureaucratic organisation and how it has been wrought at the national level. As such, national planning and urban planning have become instrumental in conveying a *noblesse oblige* notion of leadership through the making of national policies that have been proclaimed to be in the best interest of the population and produce satisfied and productive citizens. These policies had profound ramifications for the built environment in that, because there are no property taxes or other forms of tax that local municipalities can levy on local residents and businesses to fund services, except for nominal fees such as specific application processing, the municipalities must file for project funding from the central government, obliging them to follow the central government's development plans.[10] As the decades unfolded the government assumed a larger role in the economy and thus the built environment was based on a centralised planning mechanism.

National and urban planning has developed in overlapping stages. They include (1) the introduction of legislative urban growth controls and the emergence of organised municipalities; (2) the construction and development of new towns and planned communities; (3) the emergence of city master plans and comprehensive planning; (4) comprehensive national planning and the adoption of the five-year national planning approach; and (5) the construction of new industrial towns. But first an overview of the political character and administrative structure of the government and their relation to the planning system is necessary in order to facilitate a clearer understanding of the planning practice in the Kingdom.

At the top of the policy-making structure is the king, who by definition has a great degree of control in all decisions. The king is aided by advisors and institutions, all of which form the structure of the decision-making process. The king presides over the cabinet of the government's ministers or Council of Ministers, a legislative body created in 1953. By 1975 the council comprised 23 ministers heading the various bureaucratic ministries, departments, and agencies.[11] Several ministries and government departments are vested with the responsibility of making decisions that have direct and indirect impacts on urban development. Despite the considerable purview of these ministries within the areas of their authority, the king retains the final say and the ability to bypass the system.

The emergence of concerted efforts at modern, comprehensive (national) planning activity in Saudi Arabia since the late 1960s and 1970s emanated from the government's decision to shift to a modern, diversified economic base. An executive planning board was established in 1960. A Council of Ministers resolution (number 430) mandated its replacement with the Central Planning Organisation (CPO) in 1964. The CPO was entrusted with several tasks, including carrying out economic analyses and studies; submitting periodic economic reports on the economy, economic progress and trends; and preparing the Five Year

Development Plans with estimates for implementation and forecasts, which afforded advisory assistance to the king, government ministries and independent agencies, both foreign and local. In October 1975 the CPO was elevated to the Ministry of Planning, which is endowed with various research responsibilities, including monitoring development processes and formulating the Five Year Development Plans. Designed at the central government level, these plans outline the allocation of national resources by sector and space within a time framework. These developments were a result of several previous government experiments that go back to the 1930s. The emergence of the Saudi model of urban planning reflects the Kingdom's cultural characteristics, especially its political centralism and economic affluence.

Formal, comprehensive planning began in earnest in the 1970s. The decade brought the first national Five Year Development Plan, which endowed more towns with the status of municipality, increasing the number of such settlements from 54 to 162 by 1980. In one decade the first two plans provided master plans for 72 cities. They stipulated civic beautification and infrastructure. The master plans also contained copious documents that included land use, building codes, traffic requirements and land development guidelines.

Modern urban planning *per se* in Saudi Arabia has its roots in the government's desire to improve accessibility and provide services in the holy cities of Mecca and Medina during the 1930s. These efforts took the form of street widening and improving sanitary provisions to meet the rising demand for urban space in the holy cities. The goal was to accommodate more pilgrims. Economically, pilgrimage *(hajj)* constituted a substantial component of the nascent, impoverished government treasury, providing up to one third of annual income. As oil revenues began to increase, King Abdul-Aziz in 1952 abolished the dues charged to Muslim pilgrims. Politically, these efforts were a reflection of the desire of King Abdul-Aziz (the new Najdi ruler of the holy places) to cultivate worldwide Muslim confidence in him as the new guardian of the holy sites. The king acknowledged the need to devise a system of regulations and procedures aimed at enhancing order in the built environment and monitoring growth.

Urban and regional planning in the Kingdom has evolved through two distinct eras. During the first era (1930 up to the early 1970s) urban planning in Saudi Arabia was essentially an incremental and *ad hoc* process that reacted to day-to-day problems and needs. Starting in the 1970s, the second era of urban and regional planning emphasised a kind of 'holistic approach' where plans began to be based on measures and regulations aimed at controlling growth and enhancing order and scenic qualities in the built environment. The move towards systematic urban improvement and the adoption of statutory powers over subsequent urban development presents a turning point in the urban planning process.

Chronologically the first formative era in Saudi urban planning began in 1937 when Royal Order number 8723 (20 Rajab 1357 H) heralded the government's preemptive right to the regulation of urban growth and development. It sanctioned the new 'Capital Trusteeship and Municipalities' (CTM) as the first formal statute concerning the regulation of urban growth in the holy city of Mecca. The order specified regulations, measures and procedures for guiding and monitoring new developments and beautification works conductive to scenic qualities, and designated the distribution of sellers in the souk area. It also mandated that the municipality had the right to monitor housing development, protect public spaces, widen streets and create open areas for the public. The municipalities were given the authority to develop zoning and building regulations and codes. This order was followed in 1941 by the Roads and Building Statute, which indicated the authorities' need for some form of town planning under rising pressure for physical improvements in Mecca city. 'The statute concerns itself mainly with three issues: planning procedures, building codes, zoning and the right-of-way. It was through this statute that the setback concept was introduced in Saudi Arabia with the sole objective of meeting the need for future street widening.'[12]

Along with the rise in urban growth came an increase in state intervention in urban development. By the 1950s the automobile had become a primary factor in determining the landscape of the metropolis. The process of issuing a new regulation resulted from the need to counter specific problems at a specific locality. This prompted the need for intervention: a recommendation on a problem had first to be sanctioned by the relevant ministry at the capital, whose staff, depending on the nature of the problem, might have to obtain royal approval from the Council of Ministers. Prior to the development of fully fledged specialised ministries, the municipality was responsible for various town services, such as health, road grading and water provision.

In 1962 the Council of Ministers issued resolution number 808, which delegated the task of overseeing municipal affairs to the Ministry of Interior (MI). The MI's Municipal Services Department was transferred, with the Council of Ministers resolution number 517 of Ramadan 1382/1962, to the Agency of Municipal Affairs (AMA). The AMA was entrusted with supervising the municipalities' various activities, including water and sewer systems, drainage of rain water and discharge, and was responsible for urban planning, direction and control.

Building on previous experience, the Saudi government realised the importance of urban development planning, thanks to the steadily improving economic conditions in the 1960s and, more importantly, to King Faisal's leadership forcing the governments to adopt of a comprehensive national planning process based on the Five Year Development Plans. This 'second era' of urban planning witnessed a concerted effort to deal with cities and regions with respect to national socioeconomic objectives. Along with the Five Year Development Plans, the government introduced a series of comprehensive urban and regional plans that switched planning objectives from a national to a local perspective and were increasingly spacially specific.[13]

Still, local 'plans were conceived in the context of national socioeconomic objectives spelled out in the First Five-Year Development Plan (1970–1975) and provided useful physical inputs for the public and private development programs.'[14] In light of growing concern about rapid urbanisation, the government upgraded its Deputy Ministry of Interior for Municipal Affairs to a full and independent Ministry of Municipal and Rural Affairs (MOMRA) in 1975, and the previous Directorate General of Town Planning was given the status of Deputy Ministry of Town Planning (DMTP).

MOMRA and DMTP supervised the launching of 'action master plans projects' for seven major cities in the Kingdom. Each master plan comprised 15 'technical' reports dealing with two broad topics 'background studies' and reports concerned with 'applied aspects' of urban planning, that is, the implementation phase. The DMTP requested firms to help to create planning departments to supervise implementation and feedback. In addition MOMRA, in collaboration with the United Nations, introduced a three-pronged physical planning project aimed at developing a national spatial strategy.

The most comprehensive national planning effort is outlined in the fifth Five Year Development Plan.[15] The Saudi planning system is predicated on a 'philosophy of achieving economic and social development within the framework of a free market economy based on Islamic values and concepts.'[16] The emphasis on Islamic values, according to the plan, has contributed greatly to social, economic and institutional development and has been reflected in the government's preference for a free market economy. In line with Islamic commercial principles, the government has extended to the private sector full opportunities to participate in the development process. National planning activity in the Kingdom seeks to:

1. provide long-term conceptual vision to guide development;
2. provide organisational frameworks for coordinating the development efforts of the private and public sectors and to guide and initiate structural change;
3. direct government resources towards more effectively achieving long-term economic development objectives and ensuring the availability of essential public services;
4. strengthen the on-going management of the economy through periodic reviews and prepare for emerging conditions that could seriously affect the development process.[17]

Until recently the government has followed two approaches to industrial development that have had a direct impact on the formation of the contemporary built environment. The first attempts to impose zoning laws, building codes and growth controls stemmed from recognition of the need to separate urban activities into distinct zones. Land designated for industrial activity was introduced with the debut of the city master plans. Industrial space was mainly allotted for 'auxiliary' industries such as auto repair and the 'assembly industry', involving establishments specialising in the manufacture of furniture, light fixtures, fabricated metal products, and stone, clay and glass products geared towards popular demand. As cities grew, the number of these auxiliary industries increased.

In order to encourage these industries to relocate the government designated considerable areas in the least desirable sections of cities and towns as 'industrial zones'. Depending on the current theme of government development programmes, industrial establishments are offered numerous incentives, including nominal rents (one thousandth of market value) for industrial lots. In Riyadh, for example, industrial land use amounts to 3.8 per cent of the total (developed and undeveloped), in Jeddah 6.5 per cent, in Dammam 8 per cent and in Mecca 1.5 per cent. The proliferation of 'assembly industries' depends to a great extent government promotion programmes aimed at spurring growth in the industrial sector. The first such programme was not part of the effort to restructure the national economy, but rather to cater for increasing demand for services and manufactures.

The second major industry-related influence on the shaping of the contemporary built environment was the construction of two new industrial towns by the government. These multi-billion dollar projects, the oil-related industrial complexes of Jubail and Yanbu, represented a new experiment in Saudi Arabian urban and regional planning. Jubail was originally a small coastal town where fishing and pearl diving constituted the mainstay of its inhabitants. A new, massive, master-planned city was laid out in the vicinity of the quaint old town on a government-owned site of 1030 square kilometers. It is projected to house a population of 290 000 at its final developmental stage in 2010.

On the west coast the Yanbu site, occupies public land of 80 square kilometers. Yanbu, which boasted a population of 20 000 in 1977, is projected to be inhabited by 150 000 upon completion in the year 2010. The population is expected to engage mainly in the industrial complex, which has been designed to use the cheap energy made available by the construction of a 750-mile, transpeninsular pipeline bringing crude oil and natural gas from the Eastern Province. The preliminary construction costs for both towns were met by the government. Construction began in 1977 and required the importation of a large workforce. At the peak of construction activity in 1982 the number of foreign labourers exceeded 30 000. The range cost of the project includes expenditures on infrastructure and public services, industrial plants and ports as well as 33 000 housing units.[18]

The master plans of the two industrial complexes were rationalised in order to ensure the maximum functioning of the towns' urban economy, that is, industry. The two industrial complexes were organised around exploitation of the rich natural reserves of hydrocarbon and minerals and feature world-scale primary industries, as well as capital and energy-intensive manufactured products for the growing world markets. They are also designed to allow for private sector inputs primarily in to secondary and light manufacturing industries.[19]

CONCLUSION

The Saudi experiment in model industrial towns represents a milestone in the history of urban and regional planning in Saudi Arabia, with calculated emphasis on economic efficiency in tune with the economic goals stated in the Five Year Development Plans. It reflects the Saudi government's need to reap greater benefit from its natural resources in a time of high world demand. Structurally, the decision to create new towns reflects the drastic changes underlying urban growth and form. In the traditional built environment the urban form was essentially governed by local imperatives; in the modern environment policy decisions are made by the national government and are geared towards international market exigencies. The modern settlements function within a national urban network; they are a physical embodiment of the new nation-state building system.

Yet, as was the case in many developing countries whose societies underwent a massive transformation, these plans were more technical documents than realistic programmes reflecting the long-term realities of Saudi community development. A recent report by the prestigious High Commission For The Development of Arriyadh (HCDA) reads:

> Past development projects [due to rapid growth] soon became obsolete ... public utilities and other development projects were often designed and built without reliable existing data or an up-to-date systematic development strategy. Private investment in commercial and industrial projects were often made by imitation and intuition without accurate measures of the expected economic returns.[20]

This statement highlights two characteristics of the Kingdom's urban planning in particular and national planning in general. First, because urban planning remains the responsibility of central government it is essentially technical, relying on project objectives. The Saudi planning model is aimed at aiding the allocation of national resources and coordinating the activities of various government agencies in the built environment in accordance with the Five Year Development Plans. Second, because of the much touted commitment to the dictates of Islamic Shariy'ah, the state has maintained a somewhat *laissez faire* position towards local affairs and building processes. Such an attitude was evident in the structural organisation of traditional Arab Muslim towns, which comprised autonomous quarters whose internal affairs were left to the residents' discretion. Therefore modern built environments tend to reflect climatic solutions and the government's vision and affluence. All in all government planning, of which urban planning is but one facet, has been open to technically rational innovations in the allocation of national resources and the distribution of wealth.

Notes and References

1. This chapter was written by J. W. Wright, Jr., based on Dr Mubarak's PhD dissertation.
2. Michael E. Bonine, 'The Urbanization of the Persian Gulf Nations', in Alvin J. Cottrell, C. Edmund Bosworth, R. Burrell, K. McLachlan and R. M. Savory *The Persian Gulf State: A General Survey,* (Baltimore: John Hopkins University Press), p. 272. The next highest population percentage is 81 per cent in Libya: see Ervin Y. Galantay, 'Islamic Identity

and the Metropolis: the Search for Continuity', *The Proceedings of the International Conference on Urbanism in Islam*, Tokyo, Japan, 22–28 October 1989 p. 7.

3. Ahmed A. Shamekh *Spatial Patterns of Bedouin Settlement in Al-Qasim Region, Saudi Arabia*, unpublished PhD dissertation, University of Kentucky, 1975.
4. John Friedmann, 'Intention and Reality: The American Planner Overseas', *AIP Journal*, May 1969, pp. 187–94.
5. Stefano Bianca, 'The Threat to Historic Islamic Cities Through Western Style Development: The Case of The Holy City of Medina', *Islamic Quarterly*, vol. 2 (1982), p. 109.
6. Peter G. Rowe discusses this 'paradox' in his article 'Dual Aspects of Tradition in Saudi Arabian Housing Development in Setha Low and Erve Chambers *Housing Culture and Design. A Comparative Perspective* (Philadelphia: University of Pennsylvania Press, 1989), (eds), pp. 303–34.
7. Galantry, op. cit., p. 7.
8. G. Bear, 'The City', in Abdulla M. Lutfiyya and Charles Churchill (eds), *Readings in Arab Middle Eastern Socities and Culture* (Paris: Mouton, 1970), p. 641. In Saudi Arabia, all heads of municipalities are appointed by the central government.
9. Albatel, 1991.
10. It must be emphasised here that local public departments, such as the municipality, do exercise certain powers within the domain of defined operations. Local departmental agencies can press for certain exemptions or pass recommendations to their regional or national headquarters. But such requests must be ratified by high-ranking ministry executives, if not by the Council of Ministers. What is lacking is a system by which residents can exercise considerable influence on the urban process at the local community level.
11. The creation of the Council of Ministers was the final stage in King Abdul-Aziz's national consolidation of the Kingdom (Royal Decree, 9 October 1953, I Safar. 1373 H). Fouad Al-Farsy, *Saudi Arabia. A Case Study in Development* (London: KPI, 1986); Paul J. Stevens, 'The Interaction between Oil Policy and Industrial Policy in Saudi Arabia', in R. El Mallakh and D. H. El Mallakh (eds), *Saudi Arabia: Energy Developmental Planning, And Industrialization* (Lexington: Lexington Books, 1982), pp. 27–45.
12. Saleh A. Al-Hathloul and Anis-ur-Rahmaan, 'The Evolution of Urban and Regional Planning in Saudi Arabia', *Ekisrics*, no. 312 (May/June 1985), p. 206.
13. Al-Hathloul and Anis-ur-Rahmaan, op. cit., p. 206.
14. Ibid., p. 209.
15. Kingdom of Saudi Arabia, Ministry of Planning, *Fifth Development Plan* (Riyadh: 1990), p. 399.
16. Ibid, p. 3.
17. Ibid, p. 399.
18. Stuart McMinn, John Robertson and Hassan Reda, 'Socio Economic Development of the Yanbu Sub-Region. Saudi Arabia: The Impact of the Construction Workforce', *Third Planning Review*, no. 4, (November, 1983), pp. 311–32.

19. Kingdom of Saudi Arabia, *Achievements of the Development Plans: 1970–1987* (Royal Commission for Jubail and Yanbu and the Ministry of Planning, 1989).
20. Kingdom of Saudi Arabia, High Commission For The Development of Arriyadh, *Demographic Transportation Land Use And Economic Studies For The City Of Arriyadh: Executive Summary* (Riyadh, National Offset Printing Press, 1987), p. 4.

Part II

Training and Productivity in Saudi Arabia

The chapters in Part II present microeconomic reviews and examinations of issue-specific topics relating to labour, training and productivity. They collectively discuss the implications of the policies set forth by the Saudi government over the last twenty years, starting with a chapter on the private sector's managerial class in Saudi Arabia. Following this is a short chapter on the labour supply question. These are followed by chapters on managerial development, in general and with respect to small business, finance, agriculture and exporting. The two final chapters present the structure of specific industries in the Kingdom.

5 The Saudi Managerial Environment: A Review Essay and Lecture

Abdulrahman Garawi and
Mary E. Schmidt

Human resources planners must respond to the quantitative as well as the qualitative needs of an economy when deciding development strategies. Saudi Arabia's strategy for overcoming deficiencies in both the quality and quantity of human resources is well known: after decades of importing labour a policy of 'Saudisation', or replacing foreign employees with Saudi workers, is now in place. But planners must also show the same resolve to address the qualitative difficulties faced by the Kingdom's indigenous labour force. Although Saudi Arabia has been able to afford to hire expatriate employees, finance higher education for its youth and provide vocational training for workers, a higher-quality performance at the managerial level is needed to achieve continued diversification.

Before designing reform interventions it is necessary to understand the critical difficulties faced by government enterprises. Such an understanding comes from assessing the interactive elements of the public administrative system: (1) the state's role as producer and provider of goods and services; (2) the public bureaucracy as the organisational arm of the state; and (3) public management of core economic functions and delivery systems. In this chapter we elaborate on the role of management in the public administrative system through an overview of studies written by scholars on the complexities of the Saudi managerial environment. A summary of the goals of a major US–Saudi government management training programme is also provided.

FIELD STUDIES ON THE MANAGERIAL ENVIRONMENT

Centralisation and society's values and norms are the common denominators found in research undertaken by Saudi scholars in their efforts to document the decision-making process of Saudi bureaucrats. Al-Awaji, an early researcher on the Saudi managerial environment, wrote:

> Saudi Arabian society is composed of collective groups rather than of individuals and, therefore, the basic loyalty and concern of its individuals is not to the nation as a whole but to their particular collective social units which mainly centers around the family ... which provides the society with a set of basic values and conceptions which define and stimulate social interactions.[1]

In Al-Awaji's assessment, the impact of the social values environment upon bureaucratic organisation, planning and procedures has produced the following: centralisation of authority at the very top; a lack of clear-cut definitions of the duties of employees; mixtures of new and old patterns of organisation; a lack of qualified personnel, resulting in the hiring of non-Saudis; and overstaffing. The impact of the social values environment upon bureaucratic behaviour, as Al-Awaji discovered, included the immortality of time, the influence of the role of authoritarian personalities formalist aspects (subjective influence on laws, regulations and standards), the intertwining of official and social relations, promotion of the interests of a particular region or locality, resulting in the neglect of others, and favouritism when selecting government employees.

The collective nature of Saudi society injects a complicated and distinctly non-Western perspective into the Kingdom's managerial decision-making process. For example Al-Malik found that top executives and officials in business and government sectors were faced with great constraints, including external political influences, limited power and autonomy, weak systems of accountability, low organisational commitment and the absence of professional spirit among subordinates. Even though top executives in the government faced greater degrees of these constraints than their counterparts in the private sector, business firms were not necessarily more efficient than government agencies.[2]

The major strategic issues facing business organisations and affecting their efficiency were diminishing private sector dependence on government expenditure, resolving management immaturity, replacing expatriate labour; privatising government ownership of business enterprises, refining commercial jurisprudence, supporting locally manufactured products, strengthening financial institutions and markets, and promoting mutual business – government activities.

Al-Malik concluded that top business executives had many factors working in their favour when compared with government executives, such as more individual authority and power, higher salaries, more job satisfaction, less public media pressure and less political interference. Despite these favourable factors, private managers were disadvantaged by the absence of mature financial markets, an underdeveloped commercial jurisprudence system and low enforcement of accounting and marketing regulations. Entrepreneurs also lacked information about business and social behaviour, leaving strategic decision making dependent on casual observations rather than accurate forecasts.[3]

Al-Jeaid examined time utilisation among Saudi managers in the public bureaucracy to determine how efficient they were at performing administrative tasks. His findings indicated that executives were oriented towards short-range organisational planning, usually three years or less, often as short as on budget cycle. Furthermore centralisation was preventing the delegation of authority and the rationing of routine work, which in turn led to an overburdening of upper-level management. In addition, lower-level managers were underutilised, which discouraged them from taking decision-making responsibilities. Such conditions forced civil service managers to spend less time on developmental activities such as planning and human resource development.[4] Al-Shalan wrote in 1991 that Saudi managers in the public sector were influenced by religious and social norms and traditions and adopted a consultative decision-making process.[5]

The managerial characteristics described by these Saudi scholars are not unusual in public administrations that are established to keep order as opposed to those that are created to be responsive to social and economic developmental demands, although the two goals are not entirely mutually exclusive.[6] In such organisations, top-level managers can not or do not delegate their official authority to subordinates, or they do not adjust their internal programmes to improve and best utilise employees' strengths. This mechanistic approach to organisation does not serve well in turbulent circumstances because it is designed to accomplish predetermined security objectives and it causes order. An organisation that functions as a traditional organisation has difficulty in accomplishing institutional development.[7]

Another key feature of Saudi Arabia's managerial environment is that Saudi Arabia is a distributive state. Economic development literature says that institutional maturation in distributive states diverge from classic patterns of state building because bureaucracies emerged in response to the need to allocate rather than appropriate revenues.[8] Large volumes of publicly and privately controlled capital inflows that transform the tasks that bureaucratic structures are required and able to perform and precipitate the decline of regulatory and extractive institutions.

The complexities of this issue go beyond the scope of this chapter, but it is appropriate to keep in mind the following: Saudi Arabia is characteristic of a state in which extractive institutions have decayed, and bureaucracies designed exclusively to distribute revenues have assumed their place. The decline of extractive institutions has a negative impact on the long-term development of all parts of the bureaucracy as they are the base of administration, without which regulation and redistribution are impossible. Commercial and investment taxes force business managers to adopt uniform management techniques and accounting procedures.[9] Taxation also directs investment and consumption patterns. Moreover extractive, distributive and redistributive functions of the bureaucracy require different types of information gathering.[10] Because of the state's dominant role in the economy, its distributive policies and state spending, the affiliations of bureaucrats during the boom period greatly influenced social stratification and the composition of the emerging private sector. Furthermore state spending replicated tribal and regional ties within the bureaucracy and fostered both commercial and social stratification.[11]

A CRITICAL LOOK AT THE UNITED STATES–SAUDI ARABIAN JOINT ECONOMIC COMMISSION

In order to facilitate growth and efficiency in both the business class and the public administration, the Kingdom has imported a wide range of management training programmes. Many of the programmes designed by the US government for Saudi public administrators have been implemented by the United States–Saudi Arabian Joint Commission for Economic Cooperation (usually referred to as the Joint Commission, the JEC or JE Cor.). Here we will examine the JEC's training programme for the Saudi Arabian Agricultural Bank (SAAB) as it is instructive of the limitations and potential of applying a blueprint programme to managerial development in the Kingdom. Before elaborating on this programme it is important to understand some basics about the banking and business climate in Saudi Arabia. As Bandar al-Hajjar and John Presley discuss in Chapters 8 and 9 of this volume, the buoyant economic climate in the Arab Gulf from 1973–82 gave rise to potential problems for the efficiency of small businesses and problems in the loan portfolios of commercial banks. A number of underlying problems caused by this situation have now emerged:[12]

1. Rapid development initiatives created new industries for which a skilled domestic labour supply was not available. This placed a heavy reliance upon the expertise of foreign employees who lacked long-term commitment.
2. This growth also required a change in the scale of business activity – too often the typical Saudi family-owned business was unable to cope with the demands of larger-scale production because of a lack of management depth or appropriate technology.
3. There was a general lack of sophisticated financial control within business, and accounting standards had not yet been established.
4. Marketing skills were neglected as unnecessary features in a buoyant market place.

But market inefficiencies were not always the fault of suppliers of goods and services. For example a small business 'finance-gap' persisted in the private sector not because of bank indiscretions, but because businesses were reluctant to share information and because they were generally ignorant about how to structure loan applications. In short, this illustrates why training must be provided to both buyers and suppliers of financial services.

To rectify the situation, banks and businesses must continuously improve the services they provide to their clients; state-of-the-art commercial activities entail the use of more specialised staff, management structures and decision-making processes. As Azzam puts it, 'The keener competition and the shift in market orientation towards merchant banking requires a faster response time. In financial services, sophisticated management and well trained human resources are perhaps even more important that the capital of the bank.'[13]

The first SAAB programme was established by JEC in 1979 to provide 'training programs in the US for employees of the Saudi Arabian Agricultural Bank and to improve the capabilities of the Bank in the fields of management, organization, administration and economic analysis.'[14] The initial JEC–SAAB agreement covered a two-year period, at an estimated cost of $3 530 000. Fourteen years later the total project costs reached about $27 million, and the basic approach of the original programme remains intact. The SAAB programme is identified by JEC officials as one of its most successful initiatives.[15]

The SAAB training programme was jointly developed by American consultants and officials at the Saudi Arabia Agricultural Bank. The cycle for basic training of loan officers included three months of intensive English in Saudi Arabia; nine months of English in the US at a major university with a programme specific to agriculture and banking; three months of field training at branches of the US Farm Credit Bank; followed by a monitored, on-the-job training programme at SAAB to apply learned skills. The US management of this programme was done through the International Institute at the University of Evansville in Evansville, Indiana, which still provides states-side training programmes for SAAB executive trainees.

Saudi officials at SAAB selected trainees from among the lower strata of managers because of concerns over cultural sensitivities that higher-level manages would not be inclined to participate willingly. At the same time, by training managers in the lower strata bank officials felt they were increasing the capacity of future middle and higher-level managers. While training took place in the US, consultants provided SAAB with a variety of technical skills and operational systems to improve banking functions, such as development of credit and financial manuals, standardisation of forms and statistical data, and computerisation of accounting operations. An emphasis on professional ethics in financial management was put into the curriculum in order to expose people to established credit distribution practices, truth in lending policies and basic credit regulation.

More than 1600 SAAB employees have attended formal management training programmes, 535 of whom studied in the US. The plans for the coming years are to enroll SAAB employees, of which 97 per cent are Saudi, in programmes at Saudi institutes and to hold short-term management programmes in the US for senior managers.

The SAAB training programme had a noticeable impact on SAAB's institutional maturation. In the credit and financial areas, field offices reformed their procedures for processing loans, and processing time fell from 360 to 13 days. The total volume of loans increased by 59.2 per cent after the first year, and the collection of loans increased dramatically to 63.3 per cent.[16]

The SAAB system was not without diffiulties. Although a 1983 US Government Accounting Office review of JEC was generally favourable, it recommended that even more specific goals be developed. A language barrier and the use of consultants who were not trained as instructors were pinpointed as shortcomings. Furthermore many employees who received training were lured away from the bank and into flourishing opportunities in the private sector, thus SAAB did not necessarily capitalise on the training. On the positive side, trainess were probably better equipped to work in the private sector, which as alluded to earlier, was in desperate need of bettrer managers.

One of the main problems identified by the American advisors working on the SAAB development programme was a general lack of understanding of the cultural context of the Saudi management environment. For example, although the tour of duty of American consultants and administrators could be as long as five years, most people only stayed the required minimum of two years. This was not long enough to become acclimatised to the country and to establish trust between trainers, trainees and project administrators. Some Americans were not willing to adjust to the Saudi culture, and in some cases counterparts found it impossible to work together. Some Saudi officials encountered resistance within the bank because they were perceived to have adopted American attitudes and processes.

Centralisation, political influence on decision making (including the distribution of loans) and social norms greatly affected the behaviour, of SAAB employees from the perspective of Americans associated with the programme. Furthermore the programme was designed to improve the capacity of bank employees to conduct good risk analyses of loan applications, but, as explained, private business managers lacked the capacity to assess the level of assets or liabilities, structure a loan application and present a feasibility study. Small businesses lacked an understanding of the role of accounting in decision making and in obtaining institutional credit.

CONCLUSION

What does all of this mean for the future development of the Saudi Arabian managerial environment? A review of the studies of the top-level public administrators published in the late 1980s and early 1990s indicates there are still strong remnants of the traditions described by Al-Awaji in 1971, Osama in 1980, Ibrahim in 1983 and Al-Malik in 1989, that impact on the management development process. These Saudi scholars found that centralisation, temporal vision, political influence and distractions from religious and social obligations overburdened upper-level managers and led to underutilisation of lower-level managers. These factors were impediments to precise managerial decision making among development administrators and planners.

Looking at the following chapters on the banking and private small business sectors, it is clear that management in these sectors face parallel impediments: a lack of industrial standards of financial management, a dearth of forward-looking planning and hierarchical decision making within the family business. Coupled with falling oil revenues, resources have not been distributed to the medium or lower echelons of the business community. Clearly a principal goal of the Fifth Development Plan is to improve the managerial skills of the public bureaucracy, but the emphasis must penetrate the private sector if the roles and tasks of public administrators are to increase as rapidly as needed by the economy.

As development proceeds, the administrative roles and tasks of public administrators will increase steadily and rapidly, making it imperative that individuals within public administration have the capacity to handle increasing responsibilities. In Saudi Arabia, as in many developing countries, public administration constitutes development administration, for the government assumes such a major role that it becomes – in the absence of a major private sector – responsible for the development of all principal functions of the economic structure. In Saudi Arabia there has been a huge expansion in public administration's tasks and activities without due consideration of whether the manpower was available to perform such tasks. The JEC programme was an attempt to increase capacity among public sector management. Although an example of success, it also illustrates clearly that the characteristics of the Saudi managerial environment cannot be replaced by a North American blueprint.

Notes and References

1. Ibrahim Mohammed A-Awaji, 'Bureaucracy and Society in Saudi Arabia', PhD dissertation, University of Virginia, August 1971, p. 249.
2. Sulaiman M. Al-Malik, 'Strategic Decision Makers: A Study of Business and Government Top Executives in Saudi Arabia,' PhD dissertation, Georgia State University, 1989, 427.
3. Al-Malik, op. cit., pp. 416–17
4. Khalid Owaidh Al-Jeaid, 'Managerial Behavior in Saudi Arabia: Utilizing the Temporal Factor in the Analysis of Managerial Behavior (Time Management)', PhD dissertation, Florida State University, 1991.
5. Fahad Ahmed Al-Shalan, 'Participation in managerial decision-making in the Saudi Arabian public sector', PhD dissertation, University of Pittsburgh, 1991, p. 245.
6. George F. Gant, *Development Administration* (Madison: The University of Wisconsin Press, 1979).

7. See also Gareth Morgan, *Images of Organization* (London: Sage, 1986).
8. Jacques Delacroix, 'The Distributive State in the World System', *Studies in Comparative International Development*, vol. 15 (Fall 1980), pp. 3–22.
9. Lowell Harris, 'Property Taxation and Development', *Taxation and Development* (New York: Praeger, 1976).
10. See Kiren Aziz Chaudhry, 'The price of wealth: business and state in labor remittance and oil economies', *International Organization* no. 43, vol. 1 (Winter 1989): pp. 116–121. Omar El-Fataly and Richard Chackerian, 'Administration: The Forgotten suc in Arab Development', Ibrahim Ibrahim (ed), *Arab Resources* (Washington, DC: Georgetown University, Center For Contemporary Arab Studies Press, 1983)
11. Chaudhry, op. cit., pp. 116–17.
12. Bandar Al-Hajjar & John R. Presley, 'Small Business in Saudi Arabia', *Middle Eastern Studies*, vol. 28, no. 2 (April 1992), 333–51.
13. Henry T. Azzam, *The Gulf Economics in Transition* (New York: St. Martin's Press, 1988), p. 105.
14. 'U.S.–Saudi Arabia Joint Economic Commission Saudi Arabian Agricultural Bank', written agreement.
15. The original JEC agreement for SAAB stipulates that periodic reports be prepared for the project but no such reports were ever done; the Annual Report of the JEC is the closest document to an evaluation. Thus discussions with three members of the original US team, the programme director and two consultants, will be used to supplement official documents. Discussion were carried out with the first programme director (the top American field position) of the project, who stayed in his position for two years, and two of the original consultants, who remained in their positions for two and five years. All of the expenses of the project were paid by the Saudi government. At the height of the entire JEC programme, in excess of 1000 Americans were involved.
16. JEC Annual Report 1986–87.

6 Labour Constraints on Saudi Business Development

J. W. Wright, Jr, with Hani Khashoggi and Christopher Vaughn[1]

> Labor mobility is now a fact of life. migrant Managers soon may become as common as migrant workers as business globalizes and local loyalties decline.[2]

Rosenbeth Kanther's comment seems obvious enough at first; with the increased use of migrant labour there will be a greater need for migrant managers. But important changes are confronting the management of worker migration, making the 'reality of international labor a mixed and complex one.'[3] This complexity is very evident in the Arab Middle East where – contrary to Cohen's and Van Lient's notion that international labour migration began to slow down in the 1970s[4] – labour movements to the Gulf States moved against global patterns. The Kingdom became the largest regional importer of foreign labour after high oil revenues allowed it to accelerate development at a rate that could not be sustained by its indigenous workforce.[5]

As a consequence, labour importation changed the Arabs' political economy and its social hierarchies and redefined the nature of the region's strategic position. Economic liquidity in non-oil-rich countries became reliant on participation in the oil states' reinvestment of petrodollars, in hopes having been pegged on rentier-by-proxy labour export agendas.[6] Saudi Arabia and Jordan, for example, simultaneously initiated strategic migration plans, one country needing manpower, the other in desperate need of remittance income.[7] This chapter will discuss the dilemmas faced on the Saudi side of this planning equation.

The Saudi Arabian experience in planning for modernisation is unique in many ways, particularly in the speed with which economic development has taken place. Following the oil embargo in 1973 the Kingdom's ability to finance industrial development increased exponentially. The ability to accelerate capital construction brought with it mixed blessings and problems. Massive construction orders caused unprecedented levels of economic growth, but labour shortages developed in every sector and the presence of increasing numbers of foreign labour exerted inflationary pressure throughout the Kingdom's socio-economic structure.[8] Housing prices soared, food imports quadrupled, social service costs rose dramatically and local utilities failed in the face of faster than expected urbanisation.

Even today the dilemma is twofold. First, the Kingdom's population, approximately 12 million Saudi citizens spread across 700 000 square miles of land, is not large enough to support its manufacturing and service sectors.[9] The citizenry is inordinately young, 50 per cent being below the age of 15 and 70 per cent under the age of 25. Only 6 per cent of Saudi women work in the formal sectors of the economy,[10] and when Saudi women do work it is usually in family-related services.[11] Saudi men tend to benefit from the government's lucrative pension programmes and retire earlier than most. Saudi workers also tend to avoid employment in manual labour.

This is not an unusual situation in the region. The percentage of people of working age (15–64) in most Arab countries is significantly lower than in developed countries. While the percentage of working-age people in industrial economies averages around 67 per cent, the average is 55 per cent in Arab countries.[12] This is in part due to the extraordinarily high birth rates in the region, twice those in Europe.[13]

The other side to Saudi's manpower shortage problem is rooted in sectoral employment preferences. The historical oversupply of employment opportunities for indigenous workers in the Gulf region has allowed people to indulge in their aversion to labour-intensive employment, which is reinforced by the stigmas attached to vocational training programmes.[14] This has caused significant shifts in the labour market structure in the oil-rich states. There is an increasing concentration of the labour force in the service sectors, as well as significant shifts away from agriculture towards government service and management jobs.

Here we must distinguish between the rapidly developing oil-rich Arab countries, with their shortage of trained labour, and poor countries with more highly skilled labour forces that are increasing at rates that cannot be absorbed into the local economies. Another reason for the need for guest workers in Saudi Arabia stems from the Kingdom's relatively new education system. Government-funded formal educational institutions have only been open to the public since the 1960s. The mainstream acceptance of the need for education, however, is a phenomenon of the 1980s. Education is not compulsory in Saudi Arabia, although illiteracy has declined rapidly in urban areas. The best career opportunities are in vocations requiring managerial training and/or technical knowledge, and English. In recent years the Kingdom's efforts to replace foreign labour has pushed up salaries and benefits in easily attainable jobs that might otherwise have been passed over in favour of further education. As a result, 'foreign workers do much of the technical hand work, [while] Saudis serve as managers and advisors.'[15]

Thus we find thousands of expatriates coming to Saudi Arabia and other Gulf nations from northern Arab countries that are rich in technically skilled labour. The positions filled by Jordanians and Palestinians, for example, have traditionally required expert and highly specialised training, such as university professors, doctors and engineers. Manual labour has usually been imported from even poorer nations, for example Egypt and Yemen. Saudi workers have chosen to work at the middle-management level of industry and service. Agriculture, construction, engineering and maintenance are dependent by as much as 60–90 per cent or more on foreign labour, as shown in Table 6.1, compared with 8–12 per cent in 1963.[16]

The benefits of foreign labour are obvious. First, these workers solve the manpower gaps that are constraining the Saudi economy. By doing so, they increase the level of domestic production and lower the Kingdom's dependence on imported consumer goods. This adds to the amount of non-oil national revenue, which helps the economy to diversify away from its oil base. Increased productivity raises the general standard of living

Table 6.1 Development of the share of the Saudi workforce in various occupations

Occupation	*Percentage of Saudis* *1406*	*1415*
Technical and scientific	13.8	51.5
Administrative	50.1	75.1
Clerical	52.1	75.8
Sales	37.3	56.5
Services	38.1	46.5
Agriculture	73.8	89.5
Production	44.0	55.6
Machine operations	44.0	55.6
Construction	10.1	15.8

and ensures the provision of modern services. Jordanian and Palestinian teachers are largely to thank for the dramatic decline in illiteracy among Saudi youth. Moreover the presence of these workers leads to increased consumer demand and expansion of the markets for domestically produced goods and services. The regional effects of Saudi employment opportunities also gives the Kingdom enhanced political clout.

However, having so many guest workers in the work force has its price. The availability of low-wage foreign labour began to depress wages when falling oil prices in the mid-1980s forced many people to seek employment in the private sector. In effect, from the 1970s the government subsidised a two-tier national wage rate and the inability to continue such policies became economically disruptive. This wage conflict is also apparent between the employees of American and European companies, who receive the highest wages of all non-Saudi workers. Large wage differentials cause anomosity between the Saudis, Americans, Europeans and expatriate Arabs. American and European guest workers also tend to raise the level of demand for imports, putting inflationary pressure on the economy. This trend is likely to continue into the 1990s.[17]

In addition the cost of labour cannot be determined solely by measuring wages. Economic currency is lost through guest workers in two ways. The cost of support-system provision is the most immediately noticeable cost. Dependents of guest workers, especially during the second and third plan periods, caused overcrowding in schools, hospitals and other social care facilities, and they placed a strain on young infrastructure units. More expensive was the direct loss of currency through remittances to home countries. In 1973 approximately $731 million in recorded remittances flowed out of Saudi Arabia. By 1983 that figure had jumped to over half a billion dollars.[18] This drain of foreign exchange became painfully apparent following the oil price declines in 1983, and in the post Gulf War era. In spite of oil price adjustments, Saudi Arabia's deficit spending in the 1990s has led to their borrowing over one billion dollars from international money markets.[19]

Nor can the social cost of hosting a foreign workforce be overlooked. Many Saudis are worried that continued dependence on foreign workers will disturb the Islamic pattern of economy and society that is strived for in the Kingdom. Some fear that large populations of non-Muslim peoples will fuel militant religious actions that will negatively affect development. Another reason for increasing the proportion of local labour is the intention to improve representation in disparate areas of the economy.[20] To this end the government intends to reduce the amount of foreign labour to one fifth of the total population.

The roots of this Saudisation programme are found in education, its writers recognising the strong association between education and economic growth.[21] Seven universities have been established, and the enrolment of Saudi men and women has steadily increased. During this time the number of Saudi faculty members increased at an average rate of 70 members per year, as shown in Table 6.2. The number of students enrolled in universities is expected to exceed to 100 000 in the 1990s.[22] The General Organization for Technical Education and Vocational Training, the Ministry of Education and the General Presidency for Girls' Education also offer incentives to over 32 000 students to attend vocational training courses at Saudi technical colleges.[23]

Manpower planning and development have gained the attention of government. In 1980 a royal decree was issued establishing the Manpower Council, whose functions are to study the labour needs of the Kingdom and to plan and coordinate the

Table 6.2 Saudi faculty members at King Saud University, 1973–89

Year	*Full professors*	*Associate professors*	*Assistant professors*	*Total*
1973–74	1	21	75	97
1974–75	1	13	86	100
1975–76	2	14	86	102
1976–77	2	16	96	114
1977–78	4	15	128	147
1978–79	8	20	147	175
1979–80	10	26	141	177
1980–81	16	49	177	242
1981–82	20	58	193	271
1982–83	24	66	232	322
1983–84	29	75	276	280
1984–85	28	82	288	398
1985–86	28	96	318	442
1986–87	39	92	372	503
1987–88	43	120	411	574
1988–89	59	156	428	643

Source: King Saud University, 1990.

development of human resources for both public and private sectors. The importance attached to the role of the council is indicated by the fact that nine of its twelve members are representatives of the leading ministries of the Council of Ministries. The fifth plan places over 28 per cent of its budget in human resource development. This plan recognises that the quality of public service training still needs to be improved. Too little effort has been made to use training programmes borrowed from abroad or to generate indigenous ones.[24] More programmes are being developed that offer rotational assignments that are tied to training and career development.

In conclusion, the country may never entirely end its dependence on guest workers, but it may be able to encourage initiatives among the indigenous population towards more business development through private sector incentives. For now, the two sides of the oil-rich/oil-poor regional economic dynamic are complementary, but this can only be a temporary solution to the problems facing the countries on both sides. Because the Kingdom is reaching self-sufficiency in so many areas, the need for foreign labour will continue to decline and the need to plan for the integration of the young into the employ of the business sectors will become greater.

Notes and References

1. This chapter represents a blending of information presented by Dr Khashoggi and research written by Christopher Vaughn, with assistance from J. W. Wright, Jr. See Hani Khashoggi, 'Manpower Limitations and Effective Public Policy in Middle Eastern Countries', *Journal of King Saud University: Administrative Sciences*, (1410/1990) vol. 2, pp. 127–141; Marwan Abu Jaber and Christopher Vaughn, 'Jordan's Rentier-by-Proxy Economic Agenda: Recent Changes, Observations and Prospects for the Future', in *Democracy in the Middle East: Proceedings of the 1992 Annual Conference*, St Andrews; St Andrews University (1992), pp. 644–56; and Christopher Vaughn, Jordano–Saudi Labour Relations: A System of Human Capital Migration and Repatriation', BA Thesis, Washington College, 1993.
2. Rosenbeth Kanther, 'Globalism/Localism: A New Human Resource Agenda', *Harvard Business Review*, vol. 69, no. 2 (March–April 1991), p. 9.
3. Robin Cohen, *Contested Domains: Debates in International Labor Studies* (London: Zed Books, 1991), p. 4.
4. Gijsbert van Lient, 'Economic Globalization: Labour Options and Business Strategies in High Labour Cost Countries', *International Labor*, vol. 131 (1992), pp. 4–5.
5. Michael Humphrey, 'The Political Economy of Population Movements in the Middle East', *Middle East Report*, vol. 181, no. 2 (April/March 1993), pp. 2–9.
6. Frank J. Mirkow, 'The Nature of Saudi Strategic Planning: The Implications for American Foreign Policy', *The Fletcher Forum*, Winter, 1993, pp. 157–65.
7. Vaughn and Abu Jaber, op. cit.; Ataul Haq Pamanik, 'Human Resource Development in the Context of Some Resource-rich, Education Poor and Resource-poor, education-rich Developing Countries', *Economic Growth and Human Resource Development in Islamic Perspective* (Herndon, VA: International Institute for Islamic Thought, 1993). Also see J. W. Wright, 'Islamic Banking in Practice, Problems in Jordan & Saudi Arabia', The University of Durham Arab and Islamic Studies Occassional Papers Series, 1996.
8. John R. Presley and Rodney Wilson, *Banking in the Arab Gulf* (London: Macmillan, 1991), pp. 18–21.
9. Population estimates widely, ranging from 11.4 million in 'Gulf Security: The Fire Next Time?', *The Middle East*, Issue 219 (January 1993) p. 9, to 14.9 million in *Saudi Arabia: Country Profile 1992–1993*, The Economic Intelligence Unit Business International Limited, 1992),

p. 1. Presley, Wilson, Wright and others cite an approximate population of twelve million.

10. The Third Development Plan, as cited by Abdubelrasoul Ahmed Al-Ghanim, 'The Positive and Negative Aspects of the Guestworkers in Saudi Arabia and the Saudi Arabian Government's Policy Concerning Them', unpublished master's thesis, California State University, 1983, p. 4.
11. Anne Marie Weiss-Armush, ' Women in Saudi Society', in A. Al-Swcel and J. W. Wright, Jr. (eds), *Saudi Arabia: Tradition and Transition* (Michigan: Hayden-McNiel Publishers, 1993), pp. 101–117.
12. The World Bank, *World Bank Report* (New York: Oxford University Press, 1988), p. 283.
13. Ibid., pp. 222–3.
14. Birks and Sinclair, op. cit., pp. 14, 16, 21–6, 113.
15. Muhammad Suliman A. Al-Sakran, 'Factors Associated with Saudi's Participation in the Agricultural Labor Force in the Al-Zulfi Region of Saudi Arabia', unpublished master's thesis, Iowa State University, 1988), p. 3.
16. Al-Ghanim, op. cit., p. 12; Saleh Ahmed Tawi, 'The impact of Expatriate Workers on the Economy in Saudi Arabia: Compatible General Equilibrium Results', unpublished Ph.D. thesis, Oklahoma State University, (1984).
17. 'Gulf Consumer Markets in the 1990s', *Gulf Economic and Financial Report*, vol. v. (June/July 1990), p. 2.
18. Nazli, Chouri, (1986), p. 701.
19. John R. Presley, 'Development Issues in Saudi Arabia', Address to the Washington College Middle East Symposium, April 1993.
20. Glynn Cochrone, 'Politics for Strengthening Local Government in Developing Countries', *World Bank Staff Working Paper No. 584* (Washington, DC: The World Bank, 1983).
21. L. D. Stifel, *Education and Training for Public Management in Developing Countries* (New York; Rockfeller Education Foundation, 1977); S. Paul, *Managing Development Programs: The Lessons of Success* (Boulder: Westview Press, 1982; S. Paul, 'Training for Public Administration and Management in Developing Countries: A Review', *World Bank Staff Working Paper No. 584* (Washington, DC: The World Bank, 1983).
22. Kingdom of Saudi Arabia, Ministry of Higher Education, *Statistics for Higher Education 1409*, pp. 10–12.
23. The Manpower Council, Kingdom of Saudi Arabia, *The Sixth Annual Report* (Riyadh: The Manpower Council, 1989), p. 13.
24. A notable exception to this are the training programmes run by the Saudi Arabian Agricultural Bank, where low and middle management executives are sent to the United States to tour and work at farm and bank sites. These programmes, administered through the University of Evansville, are unlike the vast majority of programmes that rely on stylised academic examples rather than courses trying to solve problems.

7 Small Business in Saudi Arabia

Bandar al-Hajjar and John R. Presley[1]

The shift of emphasis towards 'small is beautiful' in developed and developing countries has been justified by both the quantitative and qualitative contribution of the small business sector to socioeconomic wellbeing. Small businesses typically account for over 90 per cent of firms and between 30 and 40 per cent of total employment (68 per cent in the case of Japan) in most developed economies.[2] A similar picture emerges in the developing world, where in most cases the proportion of total employment is much higher (60–80 per cent.)[3]

The Bolton Committee in the United Kingdom provided qualitative reasons to confirm the significant role that small businesses can play in the economy. Small businesses are the seed corn of future large businesses: they are more flexible and can adjust production more quickly to market change; and they are a source of innovation and provide opportunities for those who wish to start their own business. They produce various specialised products and services that cannot be produced economically in large quantities and they allow larger firms to concentrate on the main activities of their business by providing spare parts and other services.[4] In relation to developing countries, Stanley and Morse have stressed the importance of small businesses as a source of capital formation, particularly in an environment where investment opportunities are very limited.[5]

There is general acceptance, therefore, that small businesses can contribute significantly to the growth and expansion of the economies of both developed and developing countries. This in turn justifies the necessity of promoting small businesses to enable them to contribute effectively to the development process. The emphasis of research in both developed and developing economies has been upon the identification and extent of the small business finance gap. Much evidence has been accumulated over the years on the inability of small businesses in most sectors of the economy to finance themselves from either internal or external sources. This has led to a criticism of financial systems that fail to provide institutional finance over the short and long term to small businesses for establishment, expansion, relocation, working capital, import finance or modernisation.[6]

The empirical evidence presented here is an extension of that normally undertaken on small businesses in most countries. Its focus is not directly upon the small business finance gap,[7] but it is clearly relevant in assessing one of the possible causes of that gap, namely managerial inefficiency in small businesses in the Saudi Arabian economy, with particular reference to the wholesale and retail trade sector. The basic hypotheses to be tested here are (1) that managerial inefficiency exists in the trade sector in Saudi Arabia, and this in itself must be a constraint upon business development in the Kingdom, and (2) managerial inefficiency is a factor in the failure of small businesses in the trade sector to obtain external finance from commercial banks, semi-government development funds and other financial institutions in the Kingdom. In this latter respect the improvement of managerial efficiency may be viewed as a partial solution to solving the small business finance gap in most developing countries; the solution does not rest entirely with the creation of new financial institutions, whether public or private, nor with new credit assessment mechanisms for small businesses within existing financial institutions.

The process of transformation from one stage of economic development to the next occurs gradually as a result of the interaction of various economic and social factors. In the case of Saudi Arabia,[8] the sudden and sharp increase in oil prices during the nine years following 1973 left the government with huge financial resources, and these were allocated to a large number of economic and social projects. This accelerated the development process and required the recruitment of foreign labour and the importation of foreign goods and services (Table 7.1); the size and nature of the change in market demand necessitated the reorganisation and extension of distributive channels in the retail and wholesale trade sectors. The response of wholesalers and retailers to these structural changes was reflected in:

1. The increasing number of establishments: from 25 870 in 1971 to 66 090 in 1981 (Table 7.2).
2. The increasing number of employees: from 75 360 in 1971 to 590 886 in 1981 (Table 7.2).
3. The emergence of new distributive units, such as shopping centres, supermarkets, department stores and out-of-town centres. These units were set up in new residential areas, mainly around the cities, that had been built in response to the increasing demand for housing, mostly from the huge number of foreign workers.

In contrast to this period of rapid expansion between 1973 and 1982, from 1983 the sharp decline in oil prices, the downturn in government spending and the departure of a large number of non-Saudi workers moved the economy into a period characterised by the following:

Table 7.1 Average annual growth rate of total GDP and its components

	1964–72	*1973–81*	*1982–87*
At current prices:			
Total GDP	15.1	42.7	–10.3
Oil sector	19.7	47.3	–20.4
Non-oil sector (total)	9.2	38.5	2.5
Private	7.9	35.3	3.3
Government	13.6	44.1	–5.3
At constant prices:			
Total GDP	11.0	9.6	2.7
Oil sector	14.4	6.8	16.3
Non-oil sector (total)	6.9	14.2	1.7
Private	5.6	12.5	17.3
Government	8.7	16.1	–0.7

Sources: Various SAMA reports.

Table 7.2 Number of establishments and employees

City	*1967*	*1971*	*1976*	*1981*
Establishments:				
Riyadh	8 367	11 776	16 409	30 611
Jeddah	8 269	11 020	13 828	28 651
Dammam	2 158	3 074	4 405	6 828
Total	18 794	25 870	34 642	66 090
Employees:				
Riyadh	21 741	30 455	94 991	272 376
Jeddah	28 185	34 506	62 907	221 975
Dammam	6 733	10 399	32 670	96 535
Total	56 659	75 360	190 568	590 886

Sources: Ministry of Finance and National Economy, Central Department of Statistics, *Census of Private Establishments*, 1967, 1971, 1976 and 1981.

- Lower growth rates in many sectors and a decline in others.
- Intense competition.
- A tightened lending policy on the part of banks and development funds.
- The disappearance of abnormal profits.
- Greater fluctuation of exchange rates.

These characteristics contributed to changing the structure of the trade sector during this period. Many retailers and wholesalers were forced to diversify their businesses, move into new locations or leave the market totally.

Unfortunately there is no universally accepted definition of what constitutes a small business. The social and economic structure of each country differs, and accordingly the definition of a small business in each country embraces different criteria, that best suit its structure. The relevant statistical data are not necessarily available in all countries and therefore definitions are adopted within the constraints set by data availability.[9]

Consequently two approaches can be adopted in defining small businesses.[10] The first stresses the distinctive differential features of small and large businesses in terms of such factors as management, ownership, employment and market share. The second approach emphasises the role of statistical criteria in forming the definition, and the range of each selected criterion determines the size of the business. These criteria include such variables as number of employees, annual turnover, profits, output and capital invested. Whether the definition is on a qualitative or quantitative basis, it must be applicable, unambiguous and appropriate for the purpose of any investigation.[11]

In the context of the trade sector in Saudi Arabia, the lack of statistical data and the unwillingness of merchants to answer certain questions, particularly those relating to size of capital and turnover, left no option but to estimate the range of the chosen criteria. This differed from one trade class to another and also within the same trade classes. (The detailed nature of the definitions adopted in the study is presented in Appendix 7.1.) Essentially, retail and wholesale trade in Saudi Arabia can be divided into eight trade classes, six relate to retail trade and two to wholesale trade. These can then be subdivided by location within each city or town. They can then be classified according to annual sales and capital invested.

METHODOLOGY

The investigation outlined in this chapter was part of a much broader investigation of most small businesses in Saudi Arabia and with a much wider coverage of factors influencing small business development than managerial inefficiency. The methodology adopted, having identified small businesses in the trade sector, was to produce an unbiased sample of small businesses and to conduct a pilot study based upon interviews; the results of these in turn determined the nature of a more comprehensive questionnaire and interview study.

The sample, of necessity, had to include small businesses in each of the eight trade classes and in each of the locations identified. This was achieved partly by using the list of members of the Chambers of Commerce in each location and partly through direct distribution of questionnaires to merchants in each location. Clearly, biased results would have occurred through complete reliance on the lists of small businesses provided by the Chambers of Commerce; equally, by using a random distribution of questionnaires in each location, biased results may again have been obtained.[12] For the larger survey 313 establishments operating in different trade classes were selected; these were drawn from the membership lists of the Chambers of Commerce in Riyadh, Jeddah and Dammam. A further sample of 1304 establishments operating in different trade classes was selected randomly. Both samples were taken from the same locations.[13]

Before the main study was embarked upon a pilot study involved sending questionnaires to 72 merchants and interviewing 16 merchants. The main objectives of the pilot study were to establish a better understanding of the problems involved in small businesses and to identify new, relevant factors judged by the merchants to have great bearing on small business development, to test the response of merchants to certain questions that are considered in both developed and developing countries as being of a highly confidential nature, to get acquainted with the best approach to conducting the interviews and to determine the most suitable ways of distributing and collecting questionnaires.

Four major indications emerged from the pilot study:

1. It was apparent that lack of finance was only one factor limiting the development of small businesses.
2. The lack of management sophistication appeared to limit not only the ability (a) to approach sources of institutional finance and (b) to secure that finance, but also the general development of the business. It therefore gained much more importance than was originally intended in our broader study of small businesses in Saudi Arabia.
3. The pilot survey revealed that accounts were not readily available in small Saudi businesses. It was therefore impossible to conduct the kind of case-study approach adopted in other developing countries, based upon accounting ratios.[14] A more general approach was adopted based upon distributing a large number of questionnaires, accompanied by follow-up interviews.
4. The nature of interview techniques was also determined by the pilot study. It was found that structured interviews were

not suitable for the case of small businesses in Saudi Arabia. This was mainly due to the limited educational background among the majority of small business merchants. As a result an unstructured approach was used when interviewing merchants, which allowed for more flexibility and as little use of accounting and economic terminology as possible.

INDICATIONS OF THE QUALITY OF MANAGEMENT

This part of the questionnaire and the subsequent interviews dealing with management sophistication tested the following hypotheses. Questions were selected on the basis of their application to Saudi Arabia and their relevance in deterring managerial efficiency.[15] The following hypotheses were tested:

1. The owner-managers of small businesses have a relatively low level of education, particularly management education.
2. The majority of small businesses do not keep financial records such as bank accounts and statements, or sales, purchase, cash and payroll records.
3. The majority of small retailers and workshops do not have a separate bank account under the name of the business.
4. The majority of small businesses do not keep a proportion of their profits as a reserve.
5. The majority of small businesses do not prepare an annual budget that estimates annual sales, purchases, production, cash flow and profits.
6. Establishment of the majority of small businesses was not based on a feasibility study or a business plan.
7. The majority of entrepreneurs are not aware of the impact of high productivity on profitability, and hence on the contribution of internal funds as a source of finance.

Of the 1617 questionnaires distributed, 597 or 37 per cent were completed, collected and analysed. The breakdown of the sample is given in Table 7.3.

Table 7.3 Sample breakdown

	No. of questionnaires	*No. of respondents*	*% of R/D**	% of R/D** *sample*
Grocery wholesalers	102	40	39.2	6.7
Grocery retailers	340	129	37.9	21.5
Clothing and footwear wholesalers	58	16	27.6	2.7
Clothing and footwear retailers	420	158	37.6	26.5
Furniture and furnishing accessories retailers	86	38	44.2	6.4
Building materials retailers	400	146	36.5	24.5
Cooking utensils retailers	60	24	40.0	4.0
Consumer electronics retailers	151	46	30.5	7.7
	1617	597	36.9	100.0

$$^{*}\ \text{R/D} = \frac{\text{total questionnaires returned from each trade class}}{\text{total questionnaires distributed to each trade class}}$$

$$^{**}\text{R/S} = \frac{\text{total questionnaire returned from each trade class}}{\text{total questionnaires collected and analysed (sample)}}$$

THE RESULTS

It is postulated that merchants who have an adequate educational background, and experience and knowledge of their products and the market have easier access to institutional financial facilities than those who lack these attributes, and are generally better able to develop their businesses. This is due to their ability to apply modern techniques in management and marketing that enable them, for example, to present their case for finance in a way that convinces the financial institution of the economic viability of their projects and of the creditworthiness of the applicants. To test this empirically, the above indicators of management sophistication were used. These reflected management style, level of education, experience, and adequacy of financial information as well as the existence of a business plan or feasibility study.

The Existence of a Business Plan or Feasibility Study

A business plan or feasibility study fulfills two major functions. It allows the merchant to control and monitor the business and its performance and trends. It also allows prospective investors in the business to assess the ability of the business to succeed. The survey revealed that 95.9 per cent of merchants did not base the establishment of their business on a business plan or feasibility study. As to why business plans were not used, interviews indicated this was due to a lack of information available to the merchant, the smallness of the business not requiring such a plan, or the lack of government regulation requiring business plans to be produced. These findings therefore clearly indicate a lack of forward planning among small businesses at the inception stage.

Availability of Financial Records

After establishment, an assessment of the current financial position and forward planning depend on the availability, adequacy and reliability of the financial information and accounting records kept. Bates and Hally state that available accounting records provide entrepreneurs with the following information about their current financial position:

Table 7.4 Business plan – trade sector

Type of respondent	*Frequency*	*Per cent*	*Valid per cent*	*Cum per cent*
1	402	67.4	95.9	95.9
2	17	2.8	4.1	100.0
0	178	29.8	Missing	–
Total	597	100.0	100.0	–

Notes:
1. Respondents who do not establish their projects on the basis of a feasibility study.
2. Respondents who establish their projects on the basis of a feasibility study.
0. No answer.

1. What they are worth (that is, the difference between what they own – their assets, and what they owe – their liabilities).
2. Whether they are solvent (namely, whether they can meet their short-term liabilities from readily realisable assets).
3. Whether they have been making profit (that is, the difference between their costs and the revenue acquired from sales).
4. What they have been doing with the profit (namely, how much they have put by to maintain their assets, how much for the tax man, how much for the owners of the business, and how much for growth and security).
5. How their money has been raised and used (that is, the cash flows in their businesses).[16]

This type of information can only be obtained if entrepreneurs maintain historical accounting records, notably a balance sheet, profit and loss statement and income statement. These accounts can be forecast within a master budget, which estimates annual sales, purchases of stock or raw materials, volume of production, cash flow, profit, *zakat* (religious tax) and overall business environment. The importance of financial planning and budgeting for small businesses was expressed by Burns and Dewhurst: 'In today's rapidly changing environment small businesses are crucially vulnerable. They themselves can do little to influence that environment but must react quickly to or even anticipate, changes in it if they are to survive, never mind prosper. This is why policy and planning are so important'.[17]

In this respect, do merchants in Saudi Arabia maintain the historical and forecast accounting records that are essential for identifying their present financial position and controlling and monitoring the performance of the business in the long term? The survey found that 75.1 per cent of the respondents in the trade sector did not keep bank, sales, purchase, cash and payroll records (Table 7.5). In addition to the absence of this data, 47.4 per cent of merchants reported that they did not keep an independent bank account under the name of the establishment (Table 7.6).

Moreover 271 (91.6 per cent) of merchants did not prepare annual budgets (Table 7.7). It is clear that in the absence of this information it becomes impossible for financial institutions to apply management or project evaluation methods to assess the

Table 7.5 Financial records – trade sector

Type of respondent	*Frequency*	*Per cent*	*Valid per cent*	*Cum per cent*
1	91	15.2	24.9	24.9
2	275	46.1	75.1	100.0
0	231	38.7	Missing	–
Total	597	100.0	100.0	–

Notes:
1. Respondents who keep financial records.
2. Respondents who do not keep financial records.
0. No answer.

Table 7.6 Bank account under the name of the establishment – trade sector

Type of respondent	*Frequency*	*Per cent*	*Valid per cent*	*Cum per cent*
1	278	46.6	47.4	47.4
2	308	51.6	52.6	100.0
0	11	1.8	Missing	–
Total	597	100.0	100.0	–

Notes:
1. Businesses that have a separate bank account under the name of establishment.
2. Businesses that do not have a separate bank account under the name of establishment.
0. No answer.

creditworthiness of applicants and the ability of their projects to generate sufficient cash flow to repay their debts.

One reason for the absence of accounting records in small businesses is merchant's lack of understanding of the role of accounting in decision-making and in obtaining institutional credit. This can be attributed to many factors, including: (1) small businesses in Saudi Arabia are not required to file accounting statements; (2) inability and/or unwillingness to employ a

Table 7.7 Planning and budgeting – trade sector

Type of respondent	*Frequency*	*Per cent*	*Valid per cent*	*Cum per cent*
1	25	4.2	8.4	8.4
2	271	45.4	91.6	100.0
0	301	50.4	Missing	–
Total	596	100.0	100.0	–

Notes:
1. Businesses that prepare annual budgets.
2. Businesses that do not prepare annual budgets.
0. No answer.

qualified accountant for financial and secrecy reasons; and (3) commercial banks' lack of confidence in some accounting and auditing firms discourages them from requiring or emphasising accounting statements.

This lack of confidence is partly due to the absence of national standards for accounting and auditing. However these findings are not peculiar to Saudi Arabia – this situation is similar in both developed and developing countries, to varying degrees. For example the Bolton Committee observed that:

> Cost control and costing data are often so poor that management frequently learns of an impending crisis only with the appearance of the annual accounts or following an urgent call from the bank manager. In less serious cases, lack of costing data may make it impossible to gauge the effects on profits of different levels of activity or courses of action, especially where there is variable product mix. Credit control and stock control information is often inadequate.[18]

Bates and Hally attributed the inadequacy of accounting and financial control systems in small businesses to entrepreneurs' lack of understanding of accounting and its role in decision making:

> Many owners of small businesses are horrified by accounts of any sort, because they rarely seem to tell them very much and

hardly ever seem to have much relevance to current operations. The terminology of the accountant is precise and meaningful to the profession, but it is frequently obscure and misleading to the layman, and many owners of small businesses are simply overawed.[19]

The Degree of Experience in Business

Primarily on the grounds of confidentiality, less than 10 per cent of respondents were prepared to give details of their educational background. Of those that did respond (51), 37 per cent had not received a formal education and only 31 per cent had received a secondary school certificate. It is therefore difficult to come to a sound conclusion on educational standards among merchants. What are particularly revealing, however, are the reasons given for the establishment of the businesses (Table 7.8). Only 9.6 per cent of merchants established their businesses as a result of

Table 7.8 Main reason for undertaking the present business – trade sector

Type of respondent	*Frequency*	*Per cent*	*Valid per cent*	*Cum per cent*
1	33	5.5	9.6	9.6
2	73	12.3	21.2	30.8
3	198	33.2	57.4	88.2
4	21	3.5	6.1	94.3
5	9	1.5	2.6	96.9
6	11	1.8	3.1	100.0
0	252	42.2	Missing	
Total	597	100.0	100.0	–

Notes:
1. Experience in the field of the business.
2. High level of demand for the product of the business at the time of establishment.
3. Death or retirement of previous owner.
4. Low risk and easy to manage.
5. Lack of competition.
6. Easy supply of raw materials.
0. No answer.

previous experience in a related field of activity. In contrast 57.4 per cent had inherited their businesses after the death or retirement of the previous owners and 21 per cent of respondents regarded the high level of demand for their product(s) as the main reason for establishment.

The date of establishment of the business was clearly a key factor in the response to the question of reason for establishment. Interviews confirmed that, prior to 1973, the motive of merchants for undertaking the business was often to meet the needs and obligations of the family, especially for those who had no opportunity to continue their formal education.

These merchants secured most of their start-up capital from relatives and friends. As a result the merchant typically strove to meet family needs and to repay loans. In contrast, those who started after 1973 were motivated mostly by the perceived high returns in the private sector. They obtained start-up capital from relatives and friends who had accumulated a large amount of savings from speculation in property or from government compensation for property taken for public projects, or in some cases from government credit institutions and commercial banks.

They did not strive to achieve success like their counterparts prior to 1973. This was for two main reasons. First, the buoyant economic conditions prevailing from 1973–82 safeguarded most small businesses. Government action to accelerate the diversification process, given the low absorptive capacity of the economy, allowed even inefficient businesses to succeed and prosper.[20] Second, they had in mind that failure to repay the debt would not affect the lenders' financial position (friends, relatives). The period was marked by, for example, interest-free government loans that could be converted into grants in certain circumstances. Commercial bank loans did not have to be repaid wholly or even partially if the borrower chose to use religion as an excuse for an unwillingness or inability to repay. (There was no regulation to force borrowers to fulfill their obligations in a loan contract.) This situation meant that merchants who were only motivated by temporary abnormal returns and had a lack of adequate experience or education did not develop their managerial and marketing skills in a way that catered to the needs of the new conditions that began in 1983.

One of the common characteristics of small businesses in Saudi Arabia is that the owner is also the manager of the business: 98.1 per cent of small businesses in our sample were managed by their owners (Table 7.9). Broom and Longnecker attribute the deficiencies associated with personalised management to the inability of one individual (the owner–manager) to cope satisfactorily with all aspects of management. Small concerns in Saudi Arabia are family businesses, where the oldest member (usually male) is both founder and manager. Typically, one or two of his sons and/or brothers help him to operate the business. When he dies, or retires, the oldest member of the family succeeds him. A major problem arises because family businesses are reluctant to employ qualified outsiders, especially accountants. Furthermore they are unwilling to delegate responsibilities and authority to any family member except the oldest or the potential successor, despite the presence of others more qualified for the job in terms of experience and education. This managerial practice, which is not consistent with modern management techniques, is based on the traditions of Saudi society that emphasise age rather than ability to command respect and authority. The reluctance to employ outsiders is partly based on the belief of the owner–manager that the success of a small business depends to a large extent on secrecy and loyalty, and that these can only be maintained by family members. It also depends

Table 7.9 Management status – trade sector

Type of respondent	*Frequency*	*Per cent*	*Valid per cent*	*Cum per cent*
1	574	96.2	98.1	98.1
2	11	1.8	1.9	100.0
0	12	2.0	Missing	–
Total	597	100.0	100.0	–

Notes:
1. The owner is the manager.
2. The owner is not the manager.
0. No answer.

partly on misinterpretation of Islamic teachings, which is seen as encouraging its followers to provide financial and non-financial support to family and relatives even at the expense of inefficiency and success in business.

Use of Selling and Marketing Techniques

As an indication of basic selling and marketing techniques the questionnaire focused on whether merchants offer their customers quantity or price discounts as a method of marketing their products and avoiding delay and default in repayment. Sixty one per cent of the respondents did not offer their customers a discount for cash or early repayment (Table 7.10) However, the majority of merchants (299 or 54.6 per cent) did offer a discount to customers who purchased larger quantities of their products (Table 7.11).

Each of the indicators of managerial efficiency in small businesses in the trade sector in Saudi Arabia have offered the same conclusion: on the basis of our sample, at least, the level of management sophistication needs to be raised.[21] Given the importance of the trade sector to the Saudi economy and its role in the business development process that is underway, it is crucial that the degree of managerial efficiency is improved as a means of

Table 7.10 Quantity discount – trade sector

Type of respondent	*Frequency*	*Per cent*	*Valid per cent*	*Cum per cent*
1	299	41.7	54.6	45.4
2	249	50.1	45.4	100.0
0	49	8.2	Missing	100.0
Total	597	100.0	100.0	–

Notes:

1. Respondents who offer a discount to customers who purchase a large quantity.
2. Respondents who do not offer a discount to customers who purchase a large quantity.
0. No answer.

Table 7.11 Price discount – trade sector

Type of respondent	*Frequency*	*Per cent*	*Valid per cent*	*Cum per cent*
1	189	31.7	38.5	38.5
2	302	50.6	61.5	100.0
0	106	17.7	Missing	–
Total	597	100.0	100.0	–

Notes:
1. Respondents who offer their customers a price discount.
2. Respondents who do not offer their customers a price discount.
0. No answer.

extending the contribution of small businesses to economic development in the Kingdom.[22] It would also help to bridge the small business finance gap that exists in Saudi Arabia, despite the liquidity abundance of the last sixteen years.[23] Greater management sophistication would lead to some small businesses applying for finance from commercial banks and semi-government funding bodies in Saudi Arabia, and more financial and business information could be available up on which funding institutions could base sound financial decisions, with the risk factor involved in lending to small businesses reduced and consequently the cost of capital falling.[24]

APPENDIX 7.1 IDENTIFYING AND CLASSIFYING SMALL BUSINESSES IN THE TRADE SECTOR

First, the retail and wholesale trade sectors were divided into eight trade classes. These classes were:

1. Grocery wholesalers
2. Grocery retailers
3. Clothing and footwear wholesalers
4. Clothing and footwear retailers
5. Furniture and furnishing accessories retailers
6. Construction materials retailers

7. Cooking utensils retailers
8. Consumer electronics retailers

Of the eight classes, six relate to retail trade and only two to wholesale trade categories. In four of the six retail trade categories (furniture, building materials, consumer electronics and cooking utensils), small wholesalers do not exist. It is essential, in these sectors, for the small retailer to deal directly with the large wholesalers, who tend to be either representatives of foreign companies or distributors working on a commission basis for domestic and foreign companies.

Second, each city was divided into locations, ranging from one to four locations depending on the class of retail trade. These were:

1. Grocery retailers:
   (a) market, city centre;
   (b) main street shops;
   (c) residential areas shops.
2. Clothing and Footwear Retailers:
   (a) market, city centre;
   (b) commercial centre;
   (c) main street shops.
3. Furniture and furnishing accessories:
   (a) furniture market;
   (b) out-of-town furniture shops;
   (c) main street furniture and furnishing accessory shops.
4. Construction materials retailers:
   (a) construction material market.
5. Cooking utensils retailers:
   (a) Cooking utensils market.
6. Consumer electronics retailers:
   (a) Consumer electronics market.

The purpose behind the above division is to stress the importance of the location of the shop in determining the size of annual sales and profits, as well as the capital investment required.

Third, a sample of at least two shop owners from each location, who were classified under the same trade class, were interviewed. The interview was to estimate a range for the following criteria: annual sales, invested capital and number of employees. The results of these interviews can be summarised as follows.

Annual Sales

Grocery shop retailers:
Location 1: annual sales not exceeding SR 300 000.
Location 2: annual sales not exceeding SR 540 000.
Location 3: annual sales not exceeding SR 250 000.

Clothing and footwear retailers:
Location 1: annual sales not more than SR 720 000.
Location 2: annual sales not more than SR 540 000.
Location 3: annual sales not more than SR 360 000.
Location 4: annual sales not more than SR 200 000.

Furniture and furnishing accessories:
Location 1: annual sales not exceeding SR 1 000 000.
Location 2: annual sales not exceeding SR 500 000.
Location 3: annual sales not exceeding SR 220 000.

Construction materials:
Annuals sales not exceeding SR 2 000 000.

Cooking utensils:
Annual sales not exceeding SR 200 000.

Consumer Electronics:
Annual sales not exceeding SR 2 000 000.

Invested Capital – Retail Trade

Grocery retailers:
Location 1: capital invested not exceeding SR 200 000.
Location 2: capital invested not exceeding SR 100 000.
Location 3: capital invested not exceeding SR 100 000.

Clothing and footwear:
Location 1: capital invested not exceeding SR 300 000.

Location 2: capital invested not exceeding SR 200 000.
Location 3: capital invested not exceeding SR 150 000.
Location 4: capital invested not exceeding SR 80 000.

Furniture and furnishing accessories:
Location 1: capital invested not exceeding SR 300 000.
Location 2: capital invested not exceeding SR 200 000.
Location 3: capital invested not exceeding SR 200 000.

Construction materials retailers:
Capital invested not exceeding SR 300 000.

Cooking utensil retailers:
Capital invested not exceeding SR 150 000.

Consumer electronics retailers:
Capital invested not exceeding SR 300 000.

Wholesale Trade

Unlike the retailer, the size of the wholesaler's annual sales or capital invested is not correlated with the location of the business. In general the retailer looks for a wholesaler who sells on credit, charges lower prices than others, offers the latest styles of merchandise and is flexible, particularly in relation to the return of unsold goods. A key issue here is whether the wholesaler's ability to provide these facilities depends on the ability to obtain cheap external funds.

Notes and References

1. To come
2. Pom Ganguly, *UK Small Business Statistics and International Comparisons* (New York: Harper and Row, 1985). See also Paul Burns and Jim Dewhurst (eds), *Small Business in Europe* (London: Macmillan, 1986.
3 D. Anderson, and F. Khambata, 'Small Enterprises and Development Policy in the Philippines: A Case Study', *World Bank Staff Working Paper*, no. 468 (Washington, DC: World Bank, 1981). See also Enyinna Chuta and Carl Liedholm, *Employment and Growth in Small-Scale Industry* (London: Macmillan, 1985).
4. Bolton Report, *Report of the Committee of Inquiry on Small Firms*, Cmnd 4811 (London: HMSO, 1971).

5. E. Staley and R. Morse, *Modern Small Industry for Developing Countries* (New York: McGraw-Hill, 1965).
6. For more details on the small business financing gap in developing countries, including Nigeria, Sudan, Greece, Philippines and Sierra Leone, see the following references: Anderson and Khambata, op. cit.; R. W. Davenport, *Financing the Small Manufacturer in Developing Countries* (New York: McGraw-Hill, 1967); G. Ray and P. Hutchinson, *The Financing and Financial Control of Small Enterprise Development* (Amherst, MA: Gower, *Company*, 1983); B. E. Osaze, 'An Empirical Study of the Financing and Financial Control Characteristics of Small Rapid Growth Manufacturing Enterprises in Nigeria', PhD thesis, University of Bath, 1981; W. J. Gravin, 'The Small Business Capital Gap: The Special Case of Minority Enterprise', *Journal of Finance*, May 1971, pp. 445–57, El-Sayed Abbas Ahmed, 'An Empirical Study of the Financing of Small Enterprise Development in Sudan', PhD thesis, University of Bath; 1984 Chuta and Liedholm, op. cit.
7. Although this is part of a larger study undertaken by the authors. See B. Hajjar, 'Financing Small Businesses in Saudi Arabia', PhD thesis, Loughborough University, 1989.
8. For a general economic background see J. R. Presley and A. J. Westaway, *A Guide to the Saudi Arabian Economy*, 2nd ed. (London: Macmillan 1989).
9. For more details about the inconsistency in international statistics on small firms, see P. Burns and J. Dewhurst (eds), *Small Business in Europe* (London: Macmillan, 1986). See also Philip A. Neck, 'Role and Importance of Small Enterprises', *Small Enterprise Development: Policies and Programmes* (New York: International Labour Organization, 1977).
10. See ibid. for more details about the economic and statistical definition of small businesses. See also Bolton Report: *Report of the Committee of Inquiry on Small Firms*, Cmnd 4811 (London: HMSO, 1971). For more details about the statistical definition of small businesses in some developing countries, see Eugene Staley and Richard Morse, *Modern Small Industry for Developing Countries* (New York: McGraw-Hill, 1965).
11. These conditions were emphasised by J. R. Davies and M. Kelly, *Small Firms in the Manufacturing Sector*, Committee of Inquiry on Small Firms, Research Report No. 3, 1972.
12. Such a sample, for example, may only have included small businesses who were not members of the local Chamber of Commerce.
13. For example Kabel Street in Jeddah's downtown centre was examined; all merchants operating in this street sell cloth and footwear. The range of invested capital, annual sales and number of employees had already been estimated; this had revealed capital invested not exceeding SR 300 000, annual sales not exceeding SR 720 000 and number of employees not exceeding four. 100 questionnaires were distributed to merchants operating in this street. 17 questionnaires were handed to merchants who were members of the Jeddah Chamber of Commerce. The other 83 questionnaires were distributed randomly. The same procedure was carried out with respect to other trade classes in different locations.
14. See, for example, B. C. Osaze, and E. S. A. Ahmed, op. cit.

15. Relevance was determined by surveying management texts.
16. J. Bates and D. Hally, *The Financing of Small Business* (London: Sweet and Maxwell, 1982).
17. P. Burn and J. Dewhurst, *Small Business Planning, Finance and Control* (London: Macmillan, 1989), p. 44.
18. Bolton Report, op. cit., p. 113. See also J. Boswell, *The Rise and Decline of Small Firms* (London: George Allen & Unwin, 1972); R. Scase and R. Goffee, *The Real World of the Small Business Owner* (London: Croom Helm, 1980).
19. Bates and Hally, op. cit., p. 43.
20. J. R. Presley, 'The Impact of the Oil Recession Upon Banking in the Arab Gulf – The Need for Risk Management', *Research Paper No. 48*, Loughborough University Banking Centre March 1988.
21. H. N. Broom and J. G. Longenecker, *Small Business Management*, 4th edn (Herndon, Virginia: South-Western Publishing, 1975).
22. These results are also confirmed by a parallel study by the authors that looks at the manufacturing sector in Saudi Arabia. For details please contact the authors.
23. See J. R. Presley and A. J. Westaway, *The Saudi Arabian Economy*, 2nd edn (London: Macmillan, 1989).
24. Again evidence on this is available from the authors in a related study. See, for example, B. Al Hajjar, 'Financing Small Businesses in Saudi Arabia' (unpublished research report).

8 Attitudes, Culture and Capital Distribution in Saudi Arabia

J. W. Wright, Jr, with Bandar al-Hajjar and John R. Presley[1]

Saudi Arabia's progress towards development, and the financial structure employed to fund that progress, has created a unique economic system with many distinctive opportunities and problems. Unlike most developing economies in the last two decades, the Kingdom has vast financial resources but only modest human resources. This situation has created great pressure to import professional services, especially in the economy's financial sector where 81 per cent of personnel are foreign.[2]

Consequently a major goal of each of the Saudi Arabian government's Five Year Development Plans has been the evolution of a domestic labour pool that will decrease the Kingdom's dependency on foreign personnel. Domestically, an elaborate training system educates Saudi bankers in specialties ranging from agricultural economics to corporate finance. By providing consulting services to the Kingdom's financial institutions, agencies such as the Saudi Arabian–United States Joint Commission for Economic Cooperation organise training efforts in accounting, asset valuation, audit administration, banking, investment analysis, and risk and return profile writing. Other agencies – such as the Central Procurement and Supply Management Office, The Saudi Consulting House, the Saudi Arabian Monetary Agency, the Ministry of Finance and Economy, and the Saudi Arabian Agricultural Bank – offer specialised training programme in lending and financial services to clients and employees.[3] The expertise that has been gained through these agencies' programmes has created a new era in Gulf banking.[4]

A key component to curricula planning in financial management has been the notion that the Kingdom should base its banking structure on an Islamic economics agenda. Moreover the government has used training forums to experiment with the use of *mudaraba* and *musharaka* financing programmes as a means of further Islamicising the Kingdom's banking structure (currently not allowed for mainstream usage).[5] The government has fully realised that, given the current levels of technical and managerial know-how into the Saudi financial system, the practice of usury-free participatory financing in an economy cannot be implemented in a way that ensures optimal resource utilisation without highly trained personnel in the business sector. No matter how prepared employees in the financial sector may be, borrowers are reluctant to use Islamic financial lending.[6]

These training programmes have had mixed results. On the one hand, few governments have so generously financed infrastructure and major industrial construction. The number of operational factories increased by 154 per cent, and the number of industrial permits issued increased by 330 per cent from 1975–85. By 1987, 2016 factories had been constructed, with enough production capacity to meet at least 70 per cent of market demand. The average annual rate of real output grew by 16.6 per cent in the producing sectors, 14.1 per cent in the service sector and 4.8 per cent in the oil sector. This can be compared with an average growth rate of 2.9 per cent of GDP in the United States and 2.7 per cent in West Germany.[7]

On the other hand, the structure of the Saudi financial sector tends to undermine attempts at efficient risk management and portfolio diversification, forcing the Kingdom's banks to face levels of risk beyond those suggested by Islamic mandates. As this research points out, the risk faced by banks would be increased if *mudaraba* and *musharaka* financing were to come into mainstream use. Furthermore, as Jamshed Uppal correctly points out, the cost of financing would rise for the borrower.[8] Other writers, including Shahid, have proven theoretically that the returns to lenders would increase with the use of Islamic financial instruments. This may be true, but the reverse side is that the lender would have increased costs and higher exposure to risk. It could be argued that the business community assumes far less risk in the development process than do government-sponsored banks and financiers, a situation that is likely to increase if the issue of participatory financial instruments becomes the norm. Consequently, given the structure of banking in Saudi Arabia, the government's commitment to promoting Islamic financial practices is forcing its banks, almost by default, to bear the majority of risks through public sector banks.[9]

The crux of the problem is the absence of trained personnel in the business and financial sectors who are capable and willing to write profit profiles of firms. There is also no structure in place to guarantee consistency and conformity in business practices.[10] This chapter will investigate some of the conditions that support this assertion: (1) structural developments in the Saudi Arabian economy make risk and return profiles exceedingly difficult to establish; (2) popular attitudes towards participatory financial instruments are impeding capital distribution to the private sector; and (3) a lack of managerial sophistication in small manufacturing firms has constrained business development. Solutions to these problems may be sought through the development of a new training curriculum and nationally accepted accounting standards by the Kingdom's financial institutions.

ECONOMIC STRUCTURE AND MONETARY RISK

Economic planners in Saudi Arabia have always thought it important to develop economic structures using purely Islamic models, free from the secular regulations often imposed by Western models of development. This is particularly true in the financial sector, which has been careful to honour the Prophet's mandates against *riba* (usury), and which strives for the fair distribution of risk according to the *Sharia* (holy law). Under a completely Islamic model the banking system would therefore be based on two major forms of Islamic finance – *musharaka* financing, where both the financier and the borrower participate in a joint venture contract that includes an agreement to split losses or profits in proportion to the amount invested, and *mudaraba* financing, where one party provides the capital for a business project and a second party provides entrepreneurial and managerial skills. In the latter, profits are also shared according to a proportional contract, but in the event of bankruptcy the *mudareb* (entrepreneur) is resolved of financial responsibility because effort and time have been spent without remuneration. Islamic councils favour these methods because there are no high, up-front borrowing costs, and because they do not guarantee a return to either party. Saudi Arabian banks currently use an interest-free capital distribution system, and are experimenting with the use of equity-based financing.

As mentioned earlier, however, experiments with interest-free forms of finance have only been partially successful. The citizens of Saudi Arabia have seen more money being spent on the industrialisation and modernisation process than any other community in the world.[11] But Saudi banks may have been overly generous in interpreting their responsibilities, forcing them to accept far riskier loan portfolios than was necessary.[12] In addition, the banks' liberal lending policies make them behave more like capital venture financiers than traditional banks. A key example of this type of lending behaviour is found in the Saudi Arabian Agricultural Bank. Loans are not based on business plans or on written risk and return profiles, but instead are distributed according to each project's priority in the Kingdom's Five Year Development Plans.[13] Liberal aid, grant, and loan policies such as these have created an economic structure in which the business community controls the capital distribution process.

The fact that attempts at risk management in Saudi banking portfolios had failed became apparent in the mid-1980s, when declining oil prices forced a retrenchment of government spending.[14] This in turn revealed the business community's confusion over cash-flow management. Many business owners made no distinction between government-sponsored aid and loan receipts and cash flows provided by sales.[15] As government subsidies declined, inefficient businesses dependent on government disbursements for survival began to default on their loans. The problem became so serious in 1988 that the Real Estate Development Fund offered 20 per cent discounts for the timely repayment of loans, and an additional 10 per cent discount if repayments were made in a lump sum. By 1990, however, the system seemed to have recovered and default rates and late payments had reduced to acceptable levels.

Instead of promoting dependence on private sector profits (a stated priority in each of the Five Year Development Plans), aid and subsidy programmes may have stifled demand-based entrepreneurship and provided disincentives for profit-generated circulating capital.[16] These disincentives arise from several sources: the government's crucial role in the acquisition and distribution of productive resources,[17] the fact that the government is the country's largest consumer; the government's policy bias towards distributing funds to real estate projects; and the fact that capital circulation in Saudi Arabia involves the lending of financial resources and the borrowing of human and natural resources. Fifty-four per cent of consumption is achieved through direct government spending, and up to 75 per cent of private sector spending is supported by government-financed assistance, and by grant, loan or subsidy programmes.[18] In 1982, 56 countries had joint venture projects in Saudi Arabia, and 41 of these were contracts with the government. The service sector accounts for 66 per cent of the country's gross domestic product, 38 per cent of which comes from services provided to the government.[19] Seventy-three per cent of employment in the patriot work force is in the service sector.[20] As oil revenues declined in the late 1980s, negatively affecting real estate values, the government responded by increasing the percentage of total government credit disbursements to real-estate-intensive industries from 64 per cent to 84 per cent.[21] In addition, in 1985 possibly 80 per cent of industrial labour in the Saudi economy was foreign.[22] According to Rodney Wilson, and later according to Abdul Rehman Yousef, the system has 'a bias towards capital intensity'[23] and is based on a model in which 'imported technology is the product of an alien imagination.'[24]

This lending/borrowing relationship has been facilitated by the government's policies toward quasi-centralised procurement planning. While the intention of such policies is to keep industrial input costs low, the private sector has become inordinately attached to government funding as a source of investment cash flow, and to government purchasing agents as a source of sales. The net effect of such policies is an economy in which business revenues and asset values are more closely linked to aid and grant programmes than to corporate efficiency, and this therefore places emphasis upon the nature of risk and return in bank asset structures. Indeed, how can lending institutions create risk and return profiles if cash flows from subsidies are meant to keep inefficient businesses from failing? How can they distribute capital venture funds if businesses cannot prove the generation of non-government-linked profits? Likewise, without the threat of foreclosures the banking system becomes responsible for failing businesses' debts. This situation puts the Saudi banking structure in an unexpected and unfortunate position: it must assume most, if not all, of the Kingdom's private sector risk. To date, oil revenues have made this assumption of losses feasible, but it is a burden that the government and the banks may not be able to afford indefinitely.

ATTITUDINAL FACTORS AFFECTING RISK MANAGEMENT

While major industrial concerns seem to have taken advantage of development financing plans, small manufacturers have not done so. This is surprising given the apparent leniency of loan officers. Nevertheless only 31 per cent of the businesses that received government-backed financing employed less than thirty people, even though census reports indicate that over 91 per cent of business concerns employed less than ten persons.[25]

Clearly the small business sector is not partaking in the Kingdom's commercial lending opportunities, and a serious finance gap has developed as a result. One solution might have been to introduce *mudaraba* and *musharaka* financing programmes into the small business finance market. It should be pointed out here that we are not claiming weaknesses on the part of *mudaraba* and *musharaka* financing contracts, nor are we trying to say that there is any inherent weakness in the capital distribution systems in Islamic economic agendas. Rather we are trying to find out why Arab Muslims are not willing to participate in the Islamic banking process.[26] In the case of Saudi Arabia specifically, the reasons for this can be found in the negative attitudes of business owners towards participatory forms of financing, and in the attitude of business owners towards the management practices required for commercial sector financing.

In papers presented to the 1991 British Society of Middle Eastern Studies Conference in London, and to the 1991 International Conference on Islamic Economics in Kuala Lumpar, Bandar al-Hajjar and John R. Presley revealed an interesting phenomenon within Saudi Arabia's small business community. Completed questionnaires designed to identify private sector attitudes toward *musharaka* and *mudaraba* financing were collected from 222 small firms within Saudi Arabia's manufacturing sector (53 per cent of the questionnaires distributed were returned). The second part of the survey tried to identify the level of 'managerial sophistication' that is required to generate the types of financial data needed for banks to conduct appropriate risk and return analysis. Follow-up interviews were conducted to verify findings based on empirical data. It was found that the majority of owners of small manufacturing businesses are either unwilling or unable to accept participatory financing. One might assume that the perceived abundance of financial capital in the Saudi public sector is a source of confusion, or that it is compounding the problem. Surely many people do expect to be financially supported in a system ruled by such a rich government. But the reasons go much deeper than this: cultural values and the wish of most people to work in family-owned businesses; and the ineffective financial managerial skills of the owners of small, usually family-owned businesses in the private sector.

Eighty-three per cent of the respondents rejected the possibility of a shared financing arrangement, with only 16 per cent stating that they would willing to participate in one. Various explanations exist for this phenomenon. One is sociocultural.[27] As Louis Cantori correctly points out, Middle Eastern political and economic systems derive from a corporatist model that revolves around endogenous family relationships.[28] This often makes business leaders more concerned with support of the family than with secular profits. Researchers have found that this culturally based attachment to the family-owned business remains a factor for Arab families even after they have emigrated from the Arab world. Of the respondents, 36 per cent were more prepared to share business ownership with a friend or relative than with a financial institution or national company. Of those rejecting *musharaka* finance, the overwhelming majority (nearly 90 per cent) did so in order to remain sole owners of the business and to be in a position to hand over the business to a family member at a later date. In contrast only 13 per cent would prefer to share ownership with a commercial bank. In the six manufacturing sectors considered, rejection of *musharaka* never fell below 80 per cent in any sector, nor rose above 87.5 per cent, reflecting little sectoral variation in attitudes. Once again, family considerations were the largest concern. Others expressed concern that a new partner might assume too much control.

The *mudaraba* form of finance was only slightly more popular, with 78 per cent of respondents being unwilling to borrow in this fashion. Approximately two thirds expressed their fear that the financier would eventually take over the business. Another 30 per cent of respondents indicated that their reluctance to accept *mudaraba* was due to the fear of management interference. The surveys also indicated an unwillingness on the part of business owners to maintain separate documentation for personal and business transactions. Interviews confirmed that another reason business owners preferred to do business with family and friends was the simplicity and informality attached to it.

Taken together, these attitudes of private sector managers put lending officers in an exceedingly difficult situation. In order for banks and lending institutions to fill the small business finance gap, they must, in an Islamic economy, make participatory loans. This requires that risk and return profiles should be written on a capital venture model, one in which the financier often retains a substantial degree of executive control. But in order to encourage the business sector to participate, lenders are required by the business community to give up this influence. If we add to this the fact that loans need not be repaid if the borrower chooses to use religion as an excuse for unwillingness or inability to repay, we see a system in which the government of Saudi Arabia and the lending institutions representing the government assume inordinate amounts of risk, and in which the borrowing business community assumes little or no risk. We also see that the costs of financing and the level of risk would rise significantly if the strictest forms of *mudaraba* and *musharaka* financial instruments were commonly used. To be sure, the unwillingness of business owners to participate in risk-sharing financing is an unexpected consequence of Saudi Arabia's generous business development plans, but it is at the same time a very real consequence.

CONCLUSIONS

The crux of the problems faced by Islamic banks in the Saudi Arabian system is the lack of trained personnel in the small business and financial sectors. The problems faced by banks when lending to small businesses are exacerbated by the fact that there is no legislation requiring consistent standards of accounting, and that the commercial branch of the court system has been unable to establish and implement bankruptcy laws. While there have been a number of constitutional reforms in Saudi Arabia that should ease this situation,[29] the planned implementation of these mandates in economics and jurisprudence will not ensure the availability of appropriately trained accountants, judges, lawyers and managers. This is as much true in a capital-rich state such as Saudi Arabia as it is in a capital-poor Muslim state such as Pakistan. Wright has even argued that the problems faced by Islamic banks and foreign-styled indigenous commercial banks are essentially the same in developing Muslim Arab countries.[30] One could surmise that the economic systems in many Muslim Arab economies are so heavily biased against the lender that financial capital is virtually cost free to the individual buyer and ultimately costly to society as a whole.

The recommendations that arise with regard to this question are more evident to the training specialist than to anyone else. The ability to evaluate loans for the purposes of capital distribution relies on several factors: the adoption of a business system where managerial efficiency is taken to be the determining factor of success, and therefore the determinant of the increasing (or decreasing) value of the company; the requirement that businesses provide a consistent record of earnings; the provision for a consistent format for reporting asset values; and the development of laws providing for foreclosure and early liquidation. In order to meet these challenges the Kingdom's risk management curriculum should focus on educating borrowers in addition to training lenders. Economic literature written by Western analysts have tended to blame Islamic financial institutions when reserve deficiencies and capital shortages occur, but in so doing researchers have neglected the influence of the borrowing community in the lending process. The blame for the small business finance gap cannot be shouldered by the banks alone, even in a capital-rich economy such as Saudi Arabia. Rather the solution to the problem is multi-dimensional, involving better training in the banking system, the marketplace and the halls of government. Change in these areas can best be implemented in the following ways:

1. Through education and training – the attitude of the business community towards Islamic forms of finance must change.
2. Islamic financiers must write risk and return profiles that more accurately reflect cash flow from profits, as opposed to government subsidies; this also means that lending officers must be made fully aware of their role as capital venture examiners.
3. National accounting and reporting standards need to be developed so that borrowers can provide appropriate and consistent financial data.
4. A privatisation process should be pursued that decreases the private sector's reliance on government consumption.

At each point in this process the common denominator is training and the transfer of a permanent, indigenous managerial workforce into the financial sector, persons who are willing to become long-term members of accounting, auditing, banking and political establishments. This reminds us that the need for a skilled labour force must be combined with management of geographical, social and demographic factors to make economic progress possible. As this skilled labour force develops in the financial sector, business activity will stabilise, government policies will be defined and financial markets will become more efficient.

Notes and References

1. This chapter is a revised version of a paper written and presented by J. W. Wright, Jr on behalf of Bandar al-Hajjar and John R. Presley at the World Bank in the spring of 1993. That paper is published by the International Institute of Islamic Thought in a volume of collected proceedings entitled *Economic Growth and Human Resource Development in Islamic Perspective*. The title was changed at the request of the Information Officer at the Saudi Arabian Cultural Mission in the USA.
2. Saleh Ahmed Tawi, 'The Impact of Expatriate Workers on the Economy in Saudi Arabia: Compatible General Equilibrium Results', PhD dissertation, Oklahoma State University (1984), p. 4.
3. John R. Presley, 'The Problem of Risk Management in Banking in Oil Rich Gulf Economies', *International Journal of Bank Marketing*, vol. 1 (1992).
4. Henry T. Azzam, 'A New Era in Gulf Banking', *The Arab Gulf Journal*, vol. 5 no. 2 (October 1985), pp. 73–86; Allan C. Moore, 'Arab Banking Activities', *The Arab Gulf Journal*, vol. 5, no. 2 (October 1985), pp. 41–46.
5. For a discussion of how Islamic banks are supposed to operate in Arab countries, see *The Journal of Arab Affairs*, special edition on 'Financial Institutions in OIC Countries of the Middle East', vol. 11, pp. 1–2 (January/April 1990), which has an article on Saudi Arabian banks on pp. 207–28. See also Amal El Tigani, 'Arab Investment Companies: Types, Function and Performance', vol. 11, no. 1, (Spring 1992), pp. 34–53; Fehmy Saddy, 'The Moral Predicament of Arab Banking', vol. 5, no. 2 (Fall 1986), pp. 183–93; Rodney J. A. Wilson, 'The Role of Islamic Banks in Financial Markets', *The Arab Gulf Journal*, vol. 4, no. 2 (October 1984), pp. 53–62. Mohammad Mohsin, 'The Feasibility of Commercial Banking Without Rate of Interest', *The Islamic Quarterly,* vols. XX, XXI, XXII, no. 4 (December 1978), pp. 149–57.
6. Sadiq Abdul-Hamsed Malike, 'Institutional Inconsistency: A New Perspective in the Role of State in Development: A Case Study of Saudi Arabia', PhD dissertation, Washington University, 1991.
7. These statistics come from various Saudi government reports and are discussed in John R. Presley and Tony Westaway, *A Guide to the Saudi Arabian Economy* (London: Macmillan, 1989), pp. 9–48.
8. Jamshed Uppal, 'Investment in Human Capital Financed Under PLS Contracts', address to the Fourth International Islamic Economics Seminar on Economic Growth and Human Resource Development in Islamic Perspective. See the proceedings (Herndon, VA: International Institute of Islamic Thought, 1994), pp. 00–0.
9. Some articles that touch on the periphery of this programme are, John R. Presley, 'The Banks, Oil and the Arab Gulf Economy', *The Arab Gulf Journal*, vol. 5, no. 2 (October 1985), pp. 47–56; Ali Tawfia Sadik, 'Managing the Petrodollar Bonanza: Avenues and Implications of Recyling Arab Capital', *The Arab Gulf Journal*, vol. 6, nos 1–2, (Spring/Winter 1984), pp. 13–38; Hikmat S. Nashashi bi, 'Challenges Confronting Arab Banking', *The Arab Gulf Journal*, vol. 4, no. 2

(October 1984), pp. 63–72. Rostam M. Kauoussi, 'Economic Growth and Income Distribution in Saudi Arabia', *The Arab Gulf Journal*, vol. 5, no. 1 (Winter 1983), pp. 65–81.

10. Interview with J. Wayne Wright, Sr, former chief consultant to the Saudi Arabian Agricultural Bank (1979–82).
11. Badr I. Mohyuddin, 'Industrialization of the Arab Gulf', *Journal of Arab Affairs*, vol. 4, no. 1 (Spring 1985), pp. 47–66.
12. Henry T. Azzam, 'Investment Climate in the Gulf: Opportunities and Costraints', *The Arab Gulf Journal,* vol. 6, no. 2 (October 1986), pp. 25–36.
13. Interview with J. Wayne Wright, Sr, op. cit.
14. Rodney J. A. Wilson, 'The Impact of Reduced Oil Revenue on Arab Gulf Banking', *The Arab Gulf Journal*, vol. 6, no. 2 (October 1986), pp. 67–76, and 'The Impact of Falling Oil Revenue on Saudi Arabia's Import Policy', *The Arab Gulf Journal*, vol. 5, no. 2 (October 1985), pp. 7–16.
15. John R. Presley, 'The Problem of Risk Management in Banking in Oil Rich Gulf Economies', *International Journal of Bank Marketing*, vol. 1 (1992).
16. J. W. Wright, 'Accounting in Saudi Arabia: Imperative Questions for the 1990s', Proceedings of the 1992 British Society for Middle Eastern Studies Conference, St. Andrews University, July 1993, pp. 00–00.
17. Hashim M. Al-Ali and Yahya M. Jammal, 'Private Consumption Patterns in the Saudi Arabian Economy', *The Arab Gulf Journal*, vol. 4, no. 1 (April 1984), pp. 71–82.
18. Presley and Westaway, op. cit., p. 48.
19. Mohammed Farid Y. Kurashi, 'The Social Responsibility of the Multinational Corporations Operating in Saudi Arabia', as summarized by Constance B. Joy in Adhmed Hassan Dahlan, *Politics, Administration and Development in Saudi Arabia* (Brentwood, MD: Amana Corporation, 1990), pp. 259–77
20. John A. Shaw and Davie E. Long, *Saudi Arabia Modernization: The Impact of Change on Stability* (New York: Praeger, 1989), p. 35.
21. Presley and Westaway, op. cit., pp. 100–101, 138.
22. Population estimates vary widely, especially with respect to imported labour. Shaw and Long estimate that 80 per cent of labour is imported, but Saudi government documents put the estimate as low as 40 per cent. Typical estimates range between 60 and 80 per cent.
23. Rodney Wilson, *Banking and Finance in the Arab Middle East* (New York: St. Martin's Press, 1983), p. 63.
24. Abdul Rehman Yousef, 'The Role of Transfer of Technology in the Pursuance of Technical Progress', proceedings of a seminar organised by the Islamic Development Bank and UNCTAD on Technology Policies for Development and Selected Issues for Action (Jeddah: UNCTAD 1988) pp. 13–14.
25. Bandar al Hajjar and John R. Presley, 'Islamic Finance: Attitudes in Small Manufacturing Businesses in Saudi Arabia', *Proceedings of the International Conference on Islamic Economics* (Kuala Lumpur: International Institute for Islamic Thought, 1992).

26. Similar results have been found in studies of Muslims living in Jordan, Malaysia, Pakistan, the United Kingdom and the United States, among others.
27. Mary E. Schmidt, 'The Arab–American Family-owned Business,' *Arab–American Business and Consumer Magazine* (Washington, DC), vol. 12 (1993).
28. Louis J. Cantori, 'Corporatism, Local Politics, and Development in the Middle East', address to the Middle Eastern Studies Association (Boston, MA, 1986).
29. Rashed Aba-Namay, 'Recent Constitutional Reforms in Saudi Arabia', *International and Comparative Law Quarterly*, vol. 42, no. 2 (April 1993), pp. 295–331.
30. J. Wright, 'Islamic Banking in the Arab Middle East', address to the Middle Eastern Economics Association Conference, Washington, DC., (1993).

9 Mechanisation and Production in Saudi Agribusiness

J. W. Wright, Jr, with Salah Al-Suhaibani

Agriculture in Saudi Arabia has developed greatly in the last ten years as the government has pushed agribusiness to meet the country's demand for foodstuffs, particularly wheat. The area under cultivation increased nearly four fold between 1975 and 1987, a period when huge government support programmes were made available to farmers wanting to introduce modern agribusiness technology.[1] The Saudi Arabian Agricultural Bank (SAAB) initiated the government's incentive programmes by offering huge subsidies for those adding mechanised equipment to their capital stock. More than 29 000 subsidies were issued for tractors between 1976 and 1983.[2] Subsidy contracts for related equipment rose above 98 000. This chapter first examines the increasing mechanisation of Saudi farming and illustrates the level of modernisation achieved by comparing Saudi farms with farms in the United Kingdom and the United States. It then goes on to discuss the Saudi government's push for farm modernisation and mechanisation, resulting in increased wheat production.

A few studies on the efficiency of farm equipment and implements in Western countries are available. G. W. Krutz surveyed 46 Indiana farms to determine the overall level of mechanisation, based on tractor power and implement size per hectare.[3] He concluded that inconsistency is the rule when farmers select machinery. Another study, conducted in England, showed that wide variation exists in the mechanisation levels of farms.[4] Krutz also concluded that small farms have a tendency towards machines overcapacity on a per unit area basis.[5] The range of tractor power provisions per hectare in England is 0.87–2.98 kw; in Indiana the average is 0.97 kw.

It has been argued that modern farms in Saudi Arabia too are overmechanised. Field data about tractors and implements were collected from 56 farms in the Kingdom's central region; data were acquired about tractor power, implement width, cultivated area, soil type, and type of crops raised. All but a few farms were growing wheat at the time of the study. Most used centre pivot irrigation systems, and the common soil type was sandy loam in varying degrees. Farms were considered new if established within the last ten years. The total cultivated area of the 56 farms was 9238 hectares. The average farm area was 165 hectares, the smallest being 13 hectares and the largest 1500 hectares. The standard deviation of the farm areas was 250 hectares.

The intention of the study was to determine (1) the mechanisation level of Saudi farms, and (2) the distribution of equipment among Saudi farms. Analysis of tractor power and implement sizes are summarised in Table 9.1, alongside other data collected in the study. The average level of tractor power per hectare on Saudi farms is about double that of farms in Indiana and more than three times that of farms in Nebraska.[6] Combines used by Nebraska farmers have an average width of about one third of those used by Saudi farmers cultivating similar areas. All other implements, except bailers, were also found to be larger in Saudi Arabia than in Indiana or Nebraska.

Table 9.1 Average mechanisation provisions per hectare on modern Saudi farms compared with data from other studies

	Tractor (kW)	*Combine (m)*	*Chisel (m)*	*Moldboard (m)*	*Seed driller (m)*	*Bailer (m)*
Sum	103.065	2.447	2.781	1.085	2.513	0.953
Std	1.246	0.038	0.041	0.021	0.037	0.026
No. of obs.	56.000	48.000	53.000	42.000	53.000	38.000
Max.	6.716	0.180	0.246	0.115	0.177	0.154
Min.	0.265	0.008	0.002	0.003	0.004	0.004
Avg	1.840	0.051	0.052	0.026	0.047	0.025
USA						
Indiana (avg)	0.970	–	–	0.020	0.025	0.028
Nebraska (avg)	0.500	0.018	0.018	0.170	0.023	–

For such direct comparisons to be valid, the main parameters affecting machinery selection must be considered, including soil type and condition, relative weather patterns and necessary tillage systems. The soil type found on the Saudi farms studied varied from sandy loam to loamy sand, while the most common type of soil encountered in the Indiana and Nebraska surveys was medium textured and much heavier.[7] Tractor efficiency is low for the soil types found in Saudi Arabia, requiring more power for tractor mobility. Precipitation in the central region of Saudi Arabia is about 87 millimetres,[8] and this has a limiting effect on the number of field working days. In mid-western USA, weekly field working days range from 1.8 to 5.9 at a probability of 50 per cent.[9]

This might lead readers to conclude that, under comparable circumstances, the necessary level of mechanisation should be less in Saudi Arabia than in the United States, but in fact the studies found the opposite to be true. This may be due to the lack of Saudi experience with machinery, or to lower implement performance in the Saudi environment. The number of farm tractors and other field machines is summarised in Table 9.2. The average number of tractors per farm is 2.32, while the number of implements per farm ranges between 1.2 and 1.43. The largest number of tractors, on a farm of 1200 hectares, is six. The largest number of combines is three, chisels four, moldboards three, seed drills five and bailers three. A noticeable difference in power distribution was found among farms purchasing tractors. Inconsistency was greatest on farms cultivating 67 hectares or less. Variation

Table 9.2 Average number of agricultural machinery units among modern farms

	Tractor (kW)	*Combine (m)*	*Chisel (m)*	*Moldboard (m)*	*Seed driller (m)*	*Bailer (m)*
Sum	130.00	58.00	76.00	60.00	67.00	49.00
Std	1.14	0.50	0.71	0.58	0.70	0.45
No. of obs.	56.00	48.00	53.00	42.00	53.00	41.00
Max.	6.00	3.00	4.00	3.00	5.00	3.00
Min.	1.00	1.00	1.00	1.00	1.00	1.00
Avg	2.32	1.21	1.43	1.43	1.26	1.20

according to size of Saudi farms was similar to that reported by Krutz and Yule for American and European farms. Often, farms that had purchased a power level of 3.75 kw/per hectare or above had intended to cultivate larger areas of land, but then could not, because of the shortage of water and labour.

Even though combines are the most expensive type of mechanised equipment, 47 out of 56 Saudi farmers owned one or more. Combines were owned by farmers cultivating areas as small as 13 hectares. Larger farms showed a greater ability to match combine usage capacity to the level of production, and were therefore more efficient in their use of mechanised equipment. Bailer distribution is affected by the common practice of using part of the field for grazing, which this reduces bailing requirements.

The study of the mechanisation provisions of the 56 farms provided the following conclusions. First, while the amount of equipment purchased by Saudi farmers may be seen as excessive, the soil type, climate and water supply difficulties faced by Saudi farmers may offer a partial explanation of this. Second, we find that, where inconsistencies exist, they are in areas of production comparable to those found in Europe and the United States, that is, in the small farming community. Distribution of machinery among small farmers was not consistent with regard to tractors, chisels and moldboard ploughs, but was more equal for combines, seed drillers and bailers. Finally, the mechanical provisions among Saudi farms are much greater than those in Indiana, Nebraska and the United Kingdom. Indeed the Saudi acquisition rate for modern farm equipment per unit area is at least double that of the United States and the United Kingdom.

The benefit of this for Saudi farmers is shown by the phenomenal increase in the overall production of wheat. The country became self-sufficient in wheat in 1983 and has been producing a surplus ever since. However there have been and still are certain costs associated with this growth. The Saudi government exports its wheat surplus at the world price – almost a quarter of the domestic price it supports. In addition, increased livestock production has made Saudi Arabia one of the world's largest barley importers. This implies that the next step in Saudi agricultural development and food security plans should be a of policy of crop diversification.

In order to assess the development of wheat and its implications for overall crop production, Saudi agricultural policy, trends in the production and prices of wheat and barley, the need to promote barley production, and policy recommendations for crop diversification will be presented in the following discussion.

The Saudi agricultural sector employed 56.3 per cent of the total labour force in 1975, 48.4 per cent in 1980 and 41.9 per cent in 1987 (Table 9.3). Despite the massive economic growth that resulted from the development of the oil industry and its spillover effects into other industrial sectors, agriculture has remained one of the Kingdom's primary occupations. Overall growth in agriculture was 3.6 per cent during the first Five Year Development Plan, 5.0 per cent during the second plan and 8.1 per cent during the third plan. The agricultural sector grew by 15 per cent in 1986–87 and 16.4 per cent in 1987–88.[11] Agriculture's contribution to GDP increased from SR 2790 million in 1979–80 to SR 8652 million in 1985–86.[12] Total arable land increased by 6.7 per cent and irrigated areas increased by 13.3 per cent (Table 9.3). The notable natural challenges that Saudi farmers face deserve a second mention: water scarcity, harsh climate, sand encroachment, labour shortages, and the comparatively small size of the average land holding.[13]

Mechanisation subsidies were not the only policy pursued by the government to promote increased production. To provide an understanding of the Saudi government's support programme for agribusiness it is necessary to summarise the objectives of the Five-Year Development Plans with regard to agricultural development. The agricultural development policy had three facets: free land distribution, government subsidies and agricultural

Table 9.3 Saudi Arabian land use and agricultural labour force

	1975	*1980*	*1987*
Total land area (1000 ha)	21 4969	21 4969	21 4969
Total arable land area (1000 ha)	1035	1040	1105
Irrigated area (1000 ha)	375	390	425
Share of agricultural labour force (%)	56.3	48.8	41.9

Source: FAO Yearbook, 1989, as cited by Cakmak, p. 90.

credit. Agricultural production is a complex issue and is influenced not only by product prices, but also by conditions such as the availability and cost of inputs and the credit to purchase them; adequate prior investment in agricultural infrastructure; and farmers' confidence in the future effectiveness of price support measures. As stated, a key element of the government's agricultural programme is the free distribution of land to encourage agricultural and livestock production.[14] Under the Fallow Land Distribution Scheme, by 1980–81 98 850 hectares had been distributed to 14 554 individuals, and 60 projects in poultry breeding, dairy farming and sheep rearing had been financed. A further 955 392 hectares were distributed to 39 997 individuals and 4017 agricultural projects were started between 1980–81 and 1987. Of the land distributed up to 1986, about 68 per cent went to agribusiness projects and agricultural companies and 30 per cent to individuals (Table 9.4).

The structure of the land distribution programme reflects the government's three objectives to achieve rural development by distributing land to landless farmers; to increase efficiency by promoting large-scale farming through agricultural companies; and to increase livestock production in line with demand by encouraging investment in this sector. When the land was distributed, several difficulties arose in realizing its potential, the most serious of which was the amount of expensive irrigation and equipment required.[15] Agricultural subsidies form the cornerstone of the Kingdom's plan for addressing these problems. Programs include subsidies for wheat, rice, maize, millet and barley, and procurement subsidies for agricultural machinery and

Table 9.4 Fallow Land Distribution Scheme to the end of 1987

Beneficiary	*Number*	*Area (hectares)*
Individuals	54 551	333 959
Agri-business projects	4 077	460 349
Agricultural companies	12	259 934
Total	–	1 054 242

Source: Saudi Arabian Monetary Agency (SAMA), *Annual Report* (Riyadh: SAMA, 1988), as cited by Cakmak, p. 93.

implements – including the equipment discussed above – plus irrigation facilities, chemical fertilisers and poultry and dairy equipment.

Starting in 1973 and throughout the second plan period, government subsidies covered 45 per cent of the cost of farm machinery and 50 per cent of the cost of fertilisers. The total amount of subsidies paid to farmers rose from SR 4 million in 1973[16] to SR 1.3 billion in 1983, remained at approximately the same level up to 1985, and reduced to SR 405 million in 1986 and SR 264.5 million in 1987 (Table 9.5). Of the total subsidies disbursed during 1987–88, those for engines and pumps accounted for the largest share with 56.1 per cent. Farm machinery ranked second with 40.8 per cent, followed by cattle transport at 1.7 per cent, poultry equipment at 1.3 per cent and milk production equipment at 0.1 per cent.[17]

Next to subsidies came the distribution of development loans. The number of credit allocations steadily increased from 16 251 in 1975 to 23 758 in 1979, while the value of loans increased 378 per cent from SR 145.5 million to SR 709.1 million.[18] The number of loans reached a maximum of 38 886, and SR 4166 million in 1982, but decreased to 4792 and SR 841 million by 1987–88 (Table 9.5). Of the total loans granted in the 1987–88 period, 29.4 per cent went to agricultural projects, 20.3 per cent for the purchase of well-drilling equipment, 16.4 per cent for irri-

Table 9.5 Subsidies and loans granted by the Saudi Agricultural Bank

Year	*Loans* *Number of loans*	*Value (million SR)*	*Subsidies (million SR)*
1982/83	38 886	4166	1321.0
1983/84	23 884	3496	1023.0
1984/85	14 746	2322	1378.0
1985/86	9 209	1551	994.0
1986/87*	7 063	1019	405.0
1987/88	4 792	841	264.5

* Ten-month fiscal period.
Source: Saudi Arabian Monetary Agency (SAMA), *Annual Report*, 1987–88 (Riyadh: SAMA), as cited by Cakmak, p. 93.

gation equipment, 15.0 per cent for farm machinery, 13.6 per cent for engines and pumps and 5.3 per cent for other agricultural facilities such as greenhouses, silos and fish tanks.[19]

Taken together, mechanisation and price supports significantly increased Saudi wheat production, which averaged 160 000 tons in 1979–81 but grew by 453 per cent to reach 885 000 tons in 1983 (Table 9.6). In 1983 wheat consumption averaged 800 000 tons.

By 1985 it was clear to Saudi officials that wheat production should be levelled off and that plans for crop diversification should be implemented. The government-paid price for wheat was accordingly reduced from the SR 1016 a ton paid until 1984, to SR 571 a ton in the 1985 harvest and SR 530 a ton starting from the 1985–86 harvest (Table 9.7). However wheat output continued to rise despite the significant fall in support prices, reaching 2.135 million tons in 1984–85, a 141 per cent increase over the 1983 level. Because the Kingdom's silo capacity was about 900 000 tons at that time, the Grain Silos and Flour Mills Organisation (GSFMO) increased its storage capacity and

Table 9.6 Production and area of cereals and wheat, Saudi Arabia, 1979–88

	1979–81	*1982*	*1983*	*1984*	*1985*	*1986*	*1987*	*1988*
Production (1000 tons):								
Cereals	303	463	996	1444	2188	2461	2865	3247
Wheat	160	376	885	1068	2135	2290	2653	3000
Area harvested (1000 ha):								
Cereals	388	296	469	446	630	641	683	798
Wheat	71	157	288	404	587	566	601	680
Yield (kg/ha):								
Wheat	2254	2396	3073	2644	3637	4046	4414	4412
Share of wheat production in cereal production (%)	53	81	89	74	98	93	93	92
Share of wheat area harvested in cereal area harvested (%)	18	53	61	91	93	88	88	85

Source: FAO, *Production Yearbook*, 1984–1988, as cited by Cakmak, p. 96.

Table 9.7 Saudi and world wheat prices ($/ton)

	1983/84	*1984/85*	*1985/86*	*1986/87*
Saudi	1016	571	530	530
World*	200	185	166	142

* Import price for wheat cit. Rotterdam.
Source: IWC, World Wheat Statistics, 1987, as cited by Cakmak, p. 96.

exported 300 000 tons of the surplus (Table 9.8). Output increased again in 1986 by 7 per cent to 2.29 million tons (Table 9.6), a surplus of 1.5 million tons, and 1.6 million tons were exported (Table 9.8). Wheat output increased by another 15 per cent in 1987, reaching 2.653 million tons. In response, Saudi Arabia exported 2.4 million tons in 1987 (Table 9.8). Grain storage capacity was increased to 4.5 million tons during this period.[20] Wheat production reached a record 3.0 million tons in 1988, a growth rate of 13 per cent over 1987 levels. Exports of wheat amounted to 2.1 million tons in 1988 (Table 9.8). It is also to be noted that the wheat yield showed a substantial increase in the 1980s, from 2254 kg/ha in the 1979–81 period to 4412 kg/ha in 1988 (Table 9.6).

The percentage share of the wheat area harvested in terms of total cereals harvested averaged 18 per cent in 1979–81 and reached its maximum in 1985 with 93 per cent falling to 85 per cent in 1988 (Table 9.6). In response, current government policies are aimed at crop diversification. The government's guaran-

Table 9.8 International trade in wheat and barley (million tons)

	1985	*1986*	*1987*	*1988*	*1989*
Wheat	0.3	1.6	2.4	2.1	2.0*
Barley	−6.6	−9.0	−5.2	−4.0	−4.2*

* As at 7 July 1989.
Sources: International Wheat Council (IWC), *World Wheat Statistics, 1987; Market Report*, July, 1989, as cited by Cakmak, p. 98.

teed purchase price has been lowered for wheat since 1989 and raised for barley and other grains, except for smaller producers. Also, the GSFMO is planning to buy no more than 200 000 tons of wheat, around half of agribusiness's 1985 harvest, as a way of encouraging public companies to convert to barley production.[21]

This new focus on barley production is not only a result of the storage costs incurred by the oversupply of wheat. A large increase in imported barley has stemmed from the greater demand for meat since the oil-boom-financed increase in national income. Saudi barley production has remained below that required for meat production, and output even dropped from an average of 8000 tons during the 1979–81 period to 4000 tons in 1985 (Table 9.9). The Kingdom imported 6.6 million tons of barley that same year, and a record 9.0 million tons in 1986 (Table 9.8), making it the world's largest barley importer. Redirection of price subsidies was inevitable, and in 1986 the GSFMO set the support price for barley at SR 1000 ($267) a ton, about four times the world market price.[22] Import subsidies for barley were simultaneously decreased,[23] and were discontinued altogether in 1989.[24] As a result of the redirection of subsidies towards barley, its production increased to 121 000 tons in 1986, 162 000 tons in 1987 and 186 000 tons in 1988 (Table 9.9). This represents a saving on imports amounting to 4.0 million tons a year.

By analysing trends towards mechanisation in the Saudi Arabian's agribusiness sector, one can easily see how the country has achieved self-sufficiency in wheat. However, it is also apparent that the solution of one problem has created problems in other areas. As noted, rapid development of livestock production,

Table 9.9 Barley production in Saudi Arabia

	1979–81	*1985*	*1986*	*1987*	*1988*
Prod. of barley (1000 tons)	8	4	121	162	186
Area harvested (1000 ha)	7	2	32	43	70
Yield (kg/ha)	1143	2000	3761	3767	2657

Source: FAO, *Production Yearbook*, 1987–88, as cited by Cakmak, p. 100.

which has also been aided by mechanisation, has made the Kingdom dependent on imported barley. Past experience suggests that barley production may not increase to a level of self-sufficiency in the short term unless the price support policy is further decreased for wheat and increased for barley. In other words, a proper balance in the production of these two important crops should be achieved. Once barley production is boosted, then further redirection of subsidies may encourage the more efficient use of resources in the diversification of crop production.

Saudi Arabia has met its goals in building a physically and mechanically superior agribusiness infrastructure. This is not the same, however, as creating food security for the country. In order to achieve food security the government has to meet three conditions: production of adequate food supplies, stability in the supply flow, and access to available supplies for those who need them. Saudi Arabia, with its high per capita income, attention to food subsidies (SR 1.7 billion in 1985–86) and rural development has been and is likely to remain successful in providing food, but policy changes towards crop diversification and the optimum use of revenues in agribusiness development should be pursued.

References

1. Salah Al-Suhaibani, Mechanization Provisions of Modern Farms in Saudi Arabia, *Journal of King Saud University: Agricultural Science*, (1410/1990) vol. 2, pp. 161–169.
2. Saudi Arabian Agricultural Bank (SAAGB), 'The Bank in 20 Years', Department of Research and Studies, 1986.
3. G. W. Krutz, R. F. Combs and S. D. Parsons, 'Equipment Analysis with Farm Management Models', *Transactions of the ASAE*, vol. 23, no. 1 (1980), pp. 25–8.
4. I. Yule, T. A. Copland and G. R. O'Callaghan, 'Machinery Utilization on Arable Farms', *The Agricultural Engineer*, vol. 43, no. 1 (1988), pp. 35–9.
5. G. W. Krutz, R. F. Combs and S. D. Parsons, op. cit., pp. 25–8.
6. H. D. Jose, L. L. Bitney, D. D. Duey, L. H. Lutgen, P. E. Miller, R. E. Perry and L. F. Sheffield, *Estimated Crop and Livestock Production Costs* (Department of Agricultural Economics, Institute of Agriculture and Natural Resources, University of Nebraska-Lincoln, 1982), pp. 82–87.
7. A. Al-Darby, Personal Communcation, 1988.

8. A. A. Al-Zeid, E. U. Quintana, M. I. Abu Khate, M. N. Nimah, F. H. Alsamerai and I. I. Bashour, 'Guide for Crop Irrigation Requirements in the Kingdom of Saudi Arabia', Riyadh: FAO and Ministry of Agriculture and Water, Department of Agricultural Development, (1988).
9. D. Hunt, *Farm Power and Machinery Management*, 7th edn. (Ames: Iowa State University Press, 1979), p. 324.
10. For this discussion we have relied heavily on Malek Cakmak's work, 'Wheat Production in Saudi Arabia', *The Journal of Economic Co-operation Among Islamic Countries*, vol. 10 (1989), pp. 89–103. The data presented from here onwards has been taken from sources cited in his article.
11. Saudi Arabian Monetary Agency (SAMA), *Annual Report* (Riyadh: SAMA, 1988), pp. 20–21.
12. Ministry of Planning, Kingdom of Saudi Arabia, *Achievement of the Development Plans* (Riyadh: 1970–86), p. 13.
13. A. Tuncalp and Ugur Yavas, 'Agricultural Development in Saudi Arabia', *Third World Planning Review*, vol. 5, no. 4 (1983), pp. 334–5.
14. Ministry of Planning, Kingdom of Saudi Arabia, *Second Development Plan* (Riyadh, 1975), p. 119.
15. Ministry of Planning, Kingdom of Saudi Arabia, *Third Development Plan* (Riyadh, 1980), p. 148.
16. Ministry of Planning, Kingdom of Saudi Arabia, *Achievement of the Development Plans* (Riyadh, 1986), p. 34.
17. Ibid, p. 98.
18. Ministry of Planning, op. cit., p. 34.
19. Saudi Arabian Monetary Agency (SAMA), *Annual Report* (Riyadh: SAMA, 1988), p. 98.
20. *MEED*, vol. 33, no. 41 (1987), p. 5.
21. *MEED*, vol. 33, no. 8 (1989), p. 45.
22. *MEED*, vol. 30, no. 39 (1986), p. 30.
23. *MEED*, vol. 32, no. 6 (1988), p. 41.
24. *MEED*, vol. 33, no. 8 (1989), p. 45.

10 Saudi Arabian Export Strategy: A Micro-Level Analysis

Abdulrahman Yousef Al-Aali

Executives at export-related agencies in Saudi Arabia are trying to formulate national and regional export programmes for the Kingdom. To do this, policy makers need more information about how Saudi firms go about our exporting and what barriers we face. The reciprocal situation is that buyers in other nations wanting to purchase Saudi goods and services need to know what obstacles are faced by their suppliers. This makes the current study timely and useful as it provides policy makers at export-related agencies with a review of the current state of affairs in the Saudi private sector exporting community. This chapter will (1) examine the sectoral distribution and direction of non-petroleum exports, (2) identify obstacles faced by current exporters and ways of alleviating some of these problems, (3) profile active and sporadic exporters and (4) provide some recommendations to export promotion agencies and private sector exporters.

PREVIOUS RESEARCH

Before investigating the limitations and opportunities specific to the Saudi export environment, I will briefly review previous international research on perceived barriers to exporting. Most studies have compared exporters and non-exporters, but few have dealt with more refined subcategories such as passive, aggressive, marginal, small and medium-sized exporters. Bilkey's work is seminal because he has summarised the most frequently mentioned obstacles to exporting using these subcategories.[1] These include insufficient finances and knowledge of foreign opportunities, government restrictions, absence of access to channels of international distribution, and lack of knowledge about foreign buyers and markets. These factors were cited again in research published by Miesenbock in 1988.[2]

In 1988 Diamantopoulos and Inglis examined 13 high-involvement (aggressive) and 35 low-involvement (passive) exporters in Britain.[3] Their analysis showed that low-involvement exporters utilised a cut-off value of 50 per cent for determining the level of export intensity. Their testing through the use of multivariate analysis showed that only some variables differed statistically between the two types of exporter. Four variables showed differences: government policy, procedural and technical complexity, contextual differences, strategic limitations and local competition. Those variables that did not differ were company turnover, number of employees, company age, export experience, export assistance, internationalisation strategy, management perception of export regularity, export product base and product adaptation. Sharkey, Lim and Kim also analysed possible obstacles to exporting.[4] They found five barriers persisted throughout their research: government policy, procedural and technical complexity, contextual differences, strategic limitations and local competition.

In another study Samiee and Walters differentiated between sporadic (69 firms) and regular (62 firms) exporters.[5] The researchers pinpointed more variables that differed between the two types of exporting firms: export intensity, export volume, presence of an export department, market-oriented pricing, export market attendance, use of secondary information and number of sources used.

Three other industry-specific articles should be consulted by readers. They are Bauerschmidt, Sullivan and Gillespie's 1985 study of the global paper industry, Sullivan and Bauerschmidt's extension of that study in 1989,[6] and Gripsurd's 1990 study on Norwegian exporters.[7] The results of their research support the conclusions cited above.

As for Saudi Arabia, there were no empirical studies that examined export barriers before 1989, when I published an article comparing 83 international joint venture firms that exported with other exporters and non-exporter firms in the Kingdom.[8] I found that the average operating age of joint ventures was 7.4 years, showing that the export experience was brief among these types of manufacturer. I also reported that marked differences existed between joint venture exporters and non-exporters, using discriminate analysis. More recently Dahlan built on this work by suggesting in a paper delivered to the 1992 Gulf Chambers of Commerce's Gulf Marketing Association conference that Saudi exporters face the following obstacles: (1) lack of marketing and export experience, (2) insufficient information about foreign markets and opportunities, (3) lack of coordination between domestic manufacturers, especially in export operation and raw material import, (4) financial and legal problems when dealing with importers, (5) insufficient use of available financing programmes, (6) high local and international shipping costs and (7) increased competition in foreign markets.[9]

RESEARCH BACKGROUND AND METHODOLOGY

These barriers not withstanding, it is clear that the Kingdom intends to pursue a strong export agenda. Export diversification has become a top priority for policy makers in Saudi Arabia, and the government's drive to encourage the private sector to lead the exportation of manufactured goods is slowly being realised. The country's dependency on the export of crude oil has decreased dramatically, as evidenced by the fact that in 1991 crude oil accounted for only 78 per cent of total Saudi exports. Non-petroleum exports grew by 22 per cent annually between 1986 and 1991. In 1986 non-petroleum exports amounted to SR 4.63 billion ($1.24 billion) and rose to over SR 12.5 billion ($3.33 billion) in 1991. Non-petroleum exports accounted for 17 per cent of total Saudi exports in 1991, but were less than 1 per cent of total exports ten years earlier.[10] Table 10.1 shows that plastics, chemicals and petrochemicals account for over two thirds of total exports. The export value of these products increased threefold from $2.7 billion in 1985 to $8.9 billion in 1991. This was followed by metal products, transportation, building materials, engineering products, food and beverages, paper products, leathers and textiles, and furniture.

Table 10.1 Saudi Arabian non-petroleum exports by sector (SR million)

	1985	*1991*	*Annual growth*	*Industry share*
Plastics and chemicals	2737.4	8914.2	21.7	68.5
Metal products and transport	401.0	1069.6	17.8	8.2
Animal and agricultural products	185.0	1030.1	33.1	7.9
Building materials	47.7	609.3	52.9	4.7
Engineering products	5.9	393.9	101.4	3.0
Food and beverages	68.1	372.7	32.8	2.9
Paper products	12.9	293.5	68.3	2.3
Leather and textiles	50.2	181.8	23.9	1.4
Furniture	5.9	153.7	72.2	1.2
Total	3522.0	13 020.0	24.3	100.0

Source: *Saudi Export Directory*, 2nd edn (Riyadh: Saudi Export Development Center, 1993–4), p. 19.

As for the direction of these exports, about two thirds go to Asian nations that are not part of the Arab or Muslim world, as shown in Table 10.2. Petrochemicals represent a sizable percentage of the $4.4 billion of exports to this region. The Gulf Cooperation Council Countries (GCC) come in second place for Saudi exports, with over $3 billion. Western Europe absorbed

Table 10.2 Direction of Saudi Arabian non -mineral exports, 1991

Region	*SR million*	*% of total*
Asian countries (non-Arab, non-Islamic)	4371	33.6
GCC states	3288	25.3
Western Europe	2306	17.7
Arab League member states	1039	8.0
Non-Arab Moslem countries	849	6.5
Australia	549	6.5
North America	423	3.2
Others	195	1.5
Total	13 020	100.0

Source: *Saudi Export Directory*, 2nd edn (Riyadh: Saudi Export Development Center, 1993–4), p. 18.

17.7 per cent of Saudi exports in 1992. Other Arab League member states are the fourth largest import group, accounting for 8 per cent of Saudi exports. They are followed by the Islamic states (6.5 per cent) and Australia (4.2 per cent).

The test population used for the current study were all the manufacturing exporters who obtained certificates of origin from the Ministry of Commerce in 1992 and 1993.[11] A one-third random sample (n =148) was selected to participate in the study. A detailed questionnaire was designed that included perceived export obstacles and correlates to export activity. Nationwide interviews were conducted utilising the questionnaire, allowing for the collection of 140 usable responses.

Twenty-four obstacles were included in the survey, a larger number than had been studied in any previous research. Some of the obstacles commonly mentioned in export literature were dropped because they are irrelevant to the literature. In Saudi Arabia, for example, corporate income tax does not exist for national companies or for foreign companies during their first five to ten years of operation. A five point scale was used to measure export obstacles, with responses ranging from 'not important' (coded 1) to 'extremely important' (coded 5). The operational variables are discussed later in this chapter as the concepts are introduced. Variables deemed to have bearing on the behaviour of active and sporadic exporters were also noted. These variables represent four general strategic factors: firm and industry characteristics, export experience and organisation, export product strategy and export market strategy. For export obstacles, a five-point scale was used, the responses again ranging from 'not important' (coded 1) to 'extremely important' (coded 5). The operationalisation of other variables will be discussed when the concept is introduced.

ANALYSIS

The Sample

The sample of manufacturing firms can be described as recent exporters since 76.4 per cent of them had been exporting five years or less, as shown in Table 10.3. This is in line with the

Table 10.3 Profile of sample manufacturing exporters

Characteristic	*No. of firms*	*Per cent*
Ownership structure:		
100 per cent Saudi owned	87	62.1
Joint venture with foreign partners	53	37.9
*Firm size (revenue in SR million**):		
Up to 10	19	13.6
10 to less than 25	44	31.4
25 to less than 50	25	17.9
50 to less than 100	31	22.1
100 to less than 200	8	5.7
200 and over	13	9.3
Export experience (years):		
1–5	107	76.4
6–10	28	20.0
11–15	4	2.9
16–20	1	0.7
Industry:		
Food and beverage	30	21.4
Textile and leather	6	4.3
Paper and printing	10	7.1
Chemicals and petrochemicals	28	20.0
Plastics	18	12.9
Building materials	9	6.4
Metal products	24	17.1
Electrical products	9	6.4
Miscellaneous	6	4.3
Export performance:		
Active exporters	69	49.3
Sporadic exporters	71	50.7
Export intensity, 1987	NA	10.8
Export intensity, 1988	NA	14.7

recent growth of the manufacturing sector in Saudi Arabia. The average export/total sales ratio (export intensity) for 1992–1993 was 12.78 per cent. The revenue of 45 per cent of the sample was SR 25 million or less. An additional 40 per cent of the firms had annual revenues of over SR 25 million but less than SR 100 million. About two-fifths were in two industries: the food and beverage industry (30 exporters) and the chemical and petrochemical industry (28 exporters). The rest were in seven manufacturing industries.

Top Export Obstacles

The ten most serious obstacles to Saudi exporting are discussed in this section. It is evident from Table 10.4 that the manufacturing exporters in the sample perceived fierce competition in foreign markets ($\bar{x} = 4.12$) as the single most important obstacle facing them. Actually, 46 per cent of the respondents chose this as an extremely important obstacle. Table 10.4 further shows that absence of information about foreign markets ($\bar{x} = 3.97$) was perceived third in importance.

The second and fourth significant obstacles are somewhat related. The perception of the high cost of imported raw materials ($\bar{x} = 3.97$) and wide fluctuations in the foreign exchange rate ($\bar{x} = 3.81$) as important obstacles may signify that Saudi manufacturers depend in large part upon imported raw materials and components. Fluctuations in foreign exchange rates are very likely to affect the price of Saudi exports also.

One obstacle, high overseas transportation costs, is particularly noteworthy in the Saudi case. For example goods being shipped to East African ports just opposite Saudi Arabia (for instance from Jeddah, a major Red Sea port on the west coast) are likely to go through European or North African ports first. Few regular shipping lines operate between the lower Arabian Peninsula and Africa. Even land transportation to other Arabian Gulf countries is not cheap. The mean response to foreign shipping costs in this study ($\bar{x} = 3.6$) was the same as that in the study by Bauerschmidt, Sullivan and Gillespie.[12] Other top-ten-rated obstacles in this study were high foreign tariffs on imported products, low profitability on foreign markets, high costs of production, insufficient export financing programmes and lack of government export promotion programmes.

Active vs Sporadic Exporters

Four factors differentiating active and sporadic Saudi manufactured goods exporters are analysed in this section and summarised in Table 10.5. Active exporters are those firms seen by their executives as actively engaged in exporting and not deal-

Table 10.4 Responses to export obstacle importance

Var. no.	*Variable*	*Not at all important (1)*	*(2)*	*(3)*	*(4)*	*Extremely important (5)*	*Mean*
1.	Absence of information about foreign markets	5.7	10.7	5.0	46.4	32.1	3.89
2.	Risks involved in selling abroad	12.9	21.4	10.0	33.6	22.1	3.31
3.	Language and cultural differences	46.4	42.1	2.9	6.4	2.2	1.76
4.	Fierce competition in the foreign markets	3.6	9.3	4.3	37.1	45.7	4.12
5.	High cost of domestic transportation	10.7	25.0	5.7	39.3	19.3	3.13
6.	High overseas transportation cost	8.6	15.0	12.1	37.1	27.1	3.59
7.	Lack of productive capacity to sustain foreign demand	40.0	24.3	14.3	10.0	11.4	2.29
8.	Lack of government export promotion programmes	12.9	16.4	19.3	22.1	29.3	3.39
9.	Low profitability of foreign markets	7.9	22.1	12.1	36.4	21.4	3.41
10.	Differences of product specifications in foreign markets	19.3	31.4	9.3	28.6	11.4	2.81
11.	High storage/warehousing costs	25.0	35.0	15.0	17.1	7.9	2.48
12.	Internal operational/technical problems	41.4	33.6	5.7	13.6	5.7	2.09
13.	Complex export procedures	27.9	22.9	9.3	26.4	13.6	2.75
14.	Domestic seaport problems	31.4	28.6	17.9	13.6	8.6	2.39
15.	Confusion about foreign import regulations and procedures	18.6	22.1	20.7	24.3	14.3	2.94
16.	Management emphasis on developing domestric market	19.3	25.7	10.0	27.9	17.1	2.98
17.	Not enough export financing programmes	12.1	15.7	17.1	31.4	23.6	3.39
18.	Lack of adequate export revenue insurance	14.3	20.7	16.4	32.9	15.7	3.15
19.	High cost of production	11.4	17.9	10.7	40.0	20.0	3.39
20.	Absence of an export management and consulting company	8.6	28.0	12.1	29.3	11.4	2.86
21.	Presence of international economic integration	17.1	20.7	15.7	22.1	24.3	3.16
22.	High cost of imported raw materials	7.1	11.4	3.6	32.9	45.0	3.97
23.	Wide fluctuations in foreign exchange	7.1	12.9	8.6	35.0	36.4	3.81
24.	High foreign tariffs on imported products	16.4	8.6	12.1	37.9	25.0	3.46

Table 10.5 Differences between active and sporadic exporters in Saudi Arabia

Variables	*Active exporters*	*Sporadic exporters*	*Significant*
Firm and industry characteristics:			
Firm size (revenue, large)	43.5	31.0	No
Production capacity utilised	72.6	71.8	No
Industry technology (high-technology content)	43.5	35.2	No
Internationalisation (export initiation is result of deliberate strategy)	58.0	33.8	Yes[a]
Export profitability compared with domestic sales *(1 = much lower, 5 = much higher)*	2.63	2.40	No
Export experience and organisation:			
Export intensity (export sales/total sales)	15.7	10.0	Yes[a]
Export experience (*years*)	4.6	4.2	No
Export done in-house	92.8	93.0	No
Export department (exists separately)	20.3	7.0	Yes[b]
Full-time export staff (*number*)	2.5	1.6	Yes[b]
Export product Strategy:			
Export product base (full range exported)	50.7	47.9	No
Adapted product for export market	47.8	33.8	Yes[c]
Export market strategy:			
Export to GCC countries	98.6	95.8	No
Export to other Arab countries	53.6	39.4	Yes[c]
Export to Asian, non-Arab countries	21.7	5.6	Yes[a]
Export to African, non-Arab countries	10.1	4.2	No
Export to Europe	15.9	5.6	Yes[b]
Export to the United States	4.3	1.4	No
Geographical coverage (*number of regions covered*)	2.1	1.6	Yes[a]

Notes: Numbers are percentages unless otherwise stated. ANOVA significance level: (a) significant at 0.01 level; (b) significant at 0.05 level; (c) significant at 0.10 level.

oriented. On the other hand, sporadic exporters do not export products abroad on a regular basis.

Firm and Industry Characteristics

About 44 per cent of active exporters were considered large in size, with at least SR 50 million in annual sales. Only 31 per cent of sporadic exporters were large concerns. Both types of exporter had about 28 per cent of production capacity idle. This figure seems high and represents a capacity that could be better utilised by exporting. The two types of exporter assessed the profitability of export sales as slightly less profitable than domestic sales. This seems discouraging news for exporters. Saudi exporters are new to this international activity and may have not reached the desired level of exporting nor accumulated enough experience to reap the full benefit of exporting. This suggests that Saudi exporters should approach exporting as a long-term commitment.

Over one third of both active and sporadic exporters were in industries considered to be high-technology producers – those producing chemicals, petrochemicals and electrical products. Industries producing textiles, food and beverages, building materials, and metal products are internationally considered to be low-technology industries. This definition has no bearing on the actual technology employed by such firms.

Over half of the active exporters (58 per cent) saw their firms as having begun to export as a result of a deliberate strategy, while only one third (34 per cent) of sporadic exporters viewed themselves as strategy-directed exporters. The perceptions of both of these types of firms could be overstated, however, because this answer shows a growing importance of exporting to the Saudi private sector, which indicates the need to reach more markets to maintain growth and expansion. Firm size, export profitability, production capacity utilised and industry technology are not statistically different between the two groups of exporters. It was also observed that the strategies for internationalisation were very different between active and sporadic exporters.

Export Experience and Organisation

An important measure of export performance is export intensity (export sales as a percentage of total firm sales). For the active exporters in the sample it was 15.7 per cent while it was only 10 per cent for sporadic exporters, two markedly different figures. However the two groups are similar in that they had only a short experience of exporting – about 4.5 years.

Almost all the companies exported via the service of an in-house staff, which also meant they did not deal with export management companies or sell via foreign-owned buying offices located in Saudi Arabia. Over 20 per cent of active exporters but only 7 per cent of sporadic exporters had a separate export department. Still, the percentage of exporters with such a department was low compared with advanced countries. The two types of exporter were similar in terms of export experience and export channel (that is exporting done in-house); however they differed with regard to export intensity, the existence of an export department and the number of full-time export staff employed.

Export Product Strategy

An important dimension of a company's export position is its product strategy. Examining the product strategies of the Saudi firms in the survey makes it evident that active exporters are more likely to adapt their products for foreign buyers than are sporadic exporters (48 per cent vs 34 per cent). But in terms of the range of products manufactured and exported the two groups were not different. About half of the firms in each group exported the full range produced. The notion of product adaptation leading to more sales, as uncovered by this study, is in harmony with previously cited marketing theories.

Export Market Strategy

The second important dimension of a firm's export position is its marketing strategy. Saudi firms who are actively exporting are likely to sell their products to more regions or markets than sporadic exporters (in this study, 2.1 vs 1.6 markets). Examining the direction of exports to each region/market might add more light to Saudi's export market strategy. Table 10.5 shows that almost all the Saudi manufactured goods exporters exported to other GCC countries. Active exporters exported less to African, non-Arab and American countries, and here there was not a great difference between active and sporadic exporters. The data shows that active exporters sold to more geographical regions and to somewhat psychologically distant markets such as Asia (non-Arab) and Europe than did sporadic exporters.

RECOMMENDATIONS

This research makes three contributions to the field. First, more obstacles have been included in this study than have appeared in previous studies. Second, this research has examined the manufactured-goods exporters of a developing country, subjects that have received very little attention in the past. Third, it has identified variables that differentiate active from sporadic exporters. Recommendations to policy makers and exporters will now be presented.

Recommendations to Policy Makers Regarding Export Obstacles

Important obstacles identified in this research include fierce competition in foreign markets, the high cost of imported raw materials, the absence of information about foreign markets, high overseas transportation costs, high foreign tariffs on imported products, insufficient export financing programmes and the lack of government programmes to promote exports. This implies that both government-level and private sector-level export promotion programmes should address the export obstacles faced by active and potential international businesses. There are certain foreign-country-related obstacles that are difficult for national governments to address. Nonetheless exporters could overcome many obstacles if new government programmes were created for the benefit of exporters, and existing programmes were modified and better coordinated. Such measures would not only make government spending more effective, they would also encourage more firms to participate in exporting.

Since the majority of manufactured-goods exporters in Saudi Arabia are new to the export business, one logical government measure would be to provide potential sellers of products to overseas customers with more marketing information. Current and potential Saudi exporters need macro-level and industry-specific information about other markets, as well as practical leads. At present no governmental or quasi-governmental agency provides such a service in a systematic fashion. The Saudi Export Development Center (SEDC), part of Saudi Chamber of Commerce and Industry, tries, but does so on a very limited budget.

Another possible government programme could tackle the issue of high domestic transportation and international shipping costs. Regional shipping lines could augment large shipping companies that may not be able to send small shipments to nearby areas, such as African Red Sea ports, efficiently. In addition, some exporters need financing and insurance. At present no such support is provided by the Saudi government. While regional and multilateral programmes are available to Saudi exporters, they are not always tailored to their needs.

Recommendations to Exporters in Dealing With the Top Export Obstacles

Table 10.6 summarises the recommendations manufacturers should consider when dealing with the top five export obstacles. It should be noted that the suggestions are not comprehensive, nor are they the only alternatives. They are suggested in order to show that many marketing and business strategies, if employed in this situation, could lead to better handling of these obstacles. No matter which recommended course of action is pursued, the nature of the industry structure and its culture must always be taken into account.

It is possible that competition in foreign markets is magnified because of the short-term, deal-oriented nature of some Saudi exporters. They need to approach their exporting activities as a long-term investment and act accordingly. Reevaluating the export portfolio becomes necessary, and seeking markets receptive to Saudi goods that can command a market niche is important. Importation of raw materials did not stop the Japanese from exporting, so theoretically it should not be a problem for Saudis either. When the high cost of these materials/components is added to fluctuating exchange rates, however, the problem becomes different for Saudis. This situation is more serious for small and medium-sized Saudi exporters in particular. Searching for local substitutes,

Table 10.6 Recommendations for Saudi exporters in dealing with serious obstacles

Obstacle	*Recommendation*
Fierce competition in the foreign market	Reevaluate current markets
	Commitment to exports as a long-term investment
	Concentrate on markets that are well-selected
	Reduce production and marketing costs
	Use more promotion tools
High cost of imported raw materials	Search for local substitutes
	Try collective sourcing to increase negotiation positions
	Explore long-term commitments in order to stabilise prices
Absence of information about foreign markets	Subscribe to trade journals/reports
	Contact foreign embassies locally
	Ask proper agencies to provide needed information routinely and periodically
	Consult experts
Wide fluctuations in foreign exchange	Explore long-term commitments in order to stabilize prices
	Price using less volatile currencies
	Use foreign exchange markets to hedge
High overseas transportation cost	Use bulk forwarders
	Explore the idea of establishing private sector regional land/sea shipping companies
	Ask for government assistance when transporting on national carriers

whenever possible, is desirable. When like-manufacturers combine their sourcing, their negotiation position is enhanced. Also, entering into long-term sourcing contracts may partially remedy the situation, but admittedly it may be risky.

The absence of information about foreign opportunities is certainly an important obstacle confronting novice and small exporters. These exporters need market studies, practical information and specific leads. They can assemble secondary data from foreign embassies in Saudi Arabia about the macroeconomics and trends in their countries. Trade journals, magazines and pragmatic reports are not that expensive to obtain, and they provide statistics on many areas and sectors. In addition government and quasi-government agencies can tailor reports and studies to the circumstances of Saudi exporters. Some respondents commented that no such services are provided routinely or on a timely basis. SEDC does try to offer such information, but the need is not satisfied.

Many exporters view fluctuations in the foreign exchange rate as an important obstacle. The impact of currency movements affects both Saudi imports and Saudi exports. As discussed earlier, a large proportion of production inputs are imported. No statistics are available to document this claim; however it is plausible for several reasons. First, the Saudi industrial base and support industries are not well developed. Second, Saudi imports of intermediate goods, machinery and equipment constitute over 45 per cent of total imports.[13] This does not take into account other machinery and goods that are classified as consumer goods but can be used by manufacturers as inputs. In addition, foreign exchange fluctuations affect both importers' and exporters' long-term contractual relations with buyers, and methods for enhancing currency and exporter price stability should be explored, but with caution. In some cases certain large exporters may already be able to set prices using less volatile currencies and by hedging their revenues.

The fifth important export obstacle, as viewed by food and chemical exporters, is the high cost of overseas shipping. This obstacle can be explained when one examines the characteristics of the shipping industry that serves Saudi Arabia and its export markets. Many small exporters could coordinate their efforts with freight forwarders to consolidate small-sized shipments.

Sometimes the size of the shipment does not warrant chartering a vessel, so a strategically important step would be to establish small or regional shipping lines that could address the needs of small exporters.

Recommendations to Policy Makers Regarding Export Promotion

The current research suggests the following actions that the government and export-related agencies could take to improve the situation of exporting in Saudi Arabia.

1. Encourage new industries and manufacturing ventures, especially those industries classified as high-technology producers. This should improve export volume.
2. Encourage exports to countries dissimilar to Saudi Arabia in terms of industrial growth and/or manufacturing structure in order to minimise competition in the foreign economy. This may require the support of the government to provide detailed and practical leads in a periodic and timely manner.
3. Show the business community the importance of utilising idle capacity to increase economic development and efficiency. Full utilisation also saves precious national resources.
4. Motivate business executives and managers to pursue exporting activities because it is their managerial perceptions that most greatly impacts national export behaviour and the development of export management resources.
5. When planning export assistance, export agencies (governmental and/or quasi-governmental) may wish to examine the above results of active/sporadic exporter profiles in order to offer the most suitable and effective export promotion packages to the target group.

Recommendation to Exporters on How to Become More Active

The following recommendations to current and potential exporters are intended to be practical and straightforward in implementation.

1. A firm's size, according to the literature, may be associated with its frequency of exporting and its export performance. This research does not support that finding. Rather it suggests that size, *per se*, is not that important, but what size can bring in terms of benefits and efficiencies is important.
2. Idle productive capacity can be best used by exporting. This makes marginal costing (and not full or average cost) in export pricing an alternative and acceptable method. Marginal costing may add to profits because all, or almost all, fixed costs are already allocated to current production.
3. Export performance increases with entry into and service of multiple markets outside the traditional markets. This is especially true where the market structure is not similar to Saudi's industrial structure and/or growth expectations.
4. Management's attitudes about exporting, its profitability and regularity greatly influence export decisions and strategies. A positive attitude, as reported by previous research, develops in managers who are risk takers and have a long-term international orientation. Many of today's international developments prove that domestic-oriented firms cannot survive and expand if they do not take into consideration global developments and trends.
5. Export product adaptation or standardisation is a complex issue. Product adaptation (and other marketing programmes), which is essential to entering and/or preserving positions in important foreign markets, usually leads to increased export sales performance. But this action usually increases costs. Therefore the trade-off is to standardise the process as much as possible to contain cost and to balance it with the added benefits that come with meeting the wants and needs of more market segments.
6. Exporting's importance is highly correlated with the existence of a sufficient structure, such as an export strategy and commercial departments as well as an experienced staff.

References

1. J. W. Bilkey, 'An Attempted Integration of the Literature on the Export Behavior of Firms', *Journal of International Business Studies*, vol. 9, no. 1 (1978), pp. 33–46.

2. Kurt J. Miesenbock, 'Small Business and Exporting: A Literature Review', *International Small Business Journal*, vol. 6, no. 2 (1988), pp. 42–61.
3. A. Diamantopoulos and K. Inglis, 'Identifying differences between high and low-involvement exporters', *International Marketing Review*, vol. 5, no. 2 (1988), pp. 52–60.
4. T. W. Sharkey, J-S. Lim and K. I. Kim, 'The export involvement and preceived export barriers: An empirical analysis of small firms', *Management International Review*, vol. 29, no. 2 (1989), pp. 33–40.
5. Saeed Samiee and Peter G. P. Walters, 'Segmenting corporate exporting activities: Sporadic versus regular exporters', *Journal of the Academy of Marketing Science*, vol. 19, no. 2 (1991), pp. 93–104.
6. Alan Bauerschmidt, Daniel Sullivan, & Kate Gillespie, 'Common Factors Underlying Barriers to Exports: Studies in the U.S. Paper Industry', *Journal of International Business Studies*, vol. 16, no. 3 (1985), pp. 111–23; D. A. Sullivan and D. A. Bauerschmidt, 'Common factors underlying barriers to export: A comparative study in the European and U.S. paper industry', *Management International Review*, vol. 29, no. 2, pp. 17–32.
7. Gripsurd Geir, 'The determinants of export decisions and attitudes to a distant market: Norwegian fishery export to Japan', *Journal of International Business Studies*, vol. 231, no. 3 (1990), pp. 469–85.
8. Abdulrahman Al-Aali, 'Characteristics of exporting and nonexporting joint ventures in Saudi Arabia', *Journal of Global Marketing*, vol. 3, no. 2 (1989), pp. 61–75.
9. Abdullah Dahlan, 'The Role of Gulf Chambers of Commerce in Supporting National Exports', a paper submitted to the 4th Gulf Marketing Association, 1992.
10. Henri Azzam, 'Saudi Arabian External Trade', *Asharq Al-Awsat*, 2 December, p. 12 (1992).
11. Manufacturing Exporters, *Tegarat Al-Riyadh*, December 1988 pp. 71–3.
12. Bauerschmidt, Sullivan and Gillespie, op. cit.
13. Azzam, op. cit.

11 The Structure and Performance of Saudi Business Enterprises

M. M. Metwally and
A. M. M. Abdel-Rahman

INTRODUCTION

Very little is known about the performance of business enterprises in Saudi Arabia. This is mainly due to the lack of relevant micro-level data and to an apparent preoccupation with macroeconomic issues at the expense of some important microeconomic issues. The aim of this chapter is to use data published recently in the *Arab News* and *Al Majala* to analyse the structure of Saudi business enterprises and assess their performance.

PRELIMINARY ANALYSIS OF DATA

The *Arab News* and *Al Majala* publish information about the volume of turnover, the value of assets and the numbers employed in what the papers call 'the big 100'. Those are the 100 largest Saudi companies and business enterprises ranked by turnover and sales. This data sample covers all business enterprises whose turnover exceeded SR 232 million (approximately US$62 million) in 1991.[1] The sample covers most of the enterprises in some areas of activity and well over 80 per cent of the major enterprises in other areas. However some enterprises were excluded from the analysis due to incomplete information, such as lack of data on assets or employment.

Using the data, we classified the enterprises into eight activities, viz:

1. Finance
2. Trading and commerce
3. Contracting
4. Manufacturing
5. Public utilities, transport and communications
6. Diversified
7. Agriculture
8. Publishing and advertising

There were 22 companies in the category of diversified activities, 21 in trading and commerce, 20 in manufacturing, 13 in finance, seven in public utilities, six in contracting and two each in agriculture and publishing and advertising.

The data indicate that the majority of Saudi enterprises were established after the oil price hike in 1973. This holds for approximately 85 per cent of banks, 29 per cent of trading enterprises, 67 per cent of contracting firms, 70 per cent of manufacturing enterprises, 86 per cent of utilities and 50 per cent of diversified enterprises. This clearly shows that the oil boom had a great impact on the expansion of business activity in the Kingdom, and especially so for the more modern sectors of the economy, including finance and banking, manufacturing, contracting and utilities, compared with the more traditional sector of trading and commerce. Table 11.1 provides some statistical results on the main features of the enterprises, and suggest the following: First, the enterprises engaged in manufacturing have the highest average turnover whereas those in public utilities have the highest average employment and the second highest average turnover. Those engaged in finance have the highest average value of assets.

Second, there seems to be a strong positive correlation between the mean value of assets and the mean value of turnover, but only a weak correlation between the mean value of turnover and that of employment. The simple correlation coefficients between these variables were respectively $r_{AN} = 0.458$, $r_{QA} = 0.664$ and $r_{QN} = 0.441$, whereas the rank correlation coefficients, which avoid the influence of extreme observations, were $r_{AN} = 0.548$, $r_{QA} = 0.762$ and $r_{QN} = 0.405$, where Q refers to the mean value of turnover, A the mean value of assets and N the mean value of employment.

Table 11.1 Some basic characteristics of Saudi business enterprises

Activity	*Range*[1]	*Mean*	*Med.*[2]	*SD*[3]	*CV*[4]
Turnover:					
Finance	8590	1785.000	1171.0	2352.700	1.318
Trading and commerce	678	446.143	373.0	196.309	0.440
Contracting	1118	626.000	455.5	426.404	0.681
Manufacturing	14368	2166.400	440.0	4038.700	1.864
Public utilities	7446	1998.290	1451.0	2603.320	1.303
Diversified	9723	1595.820	735.0	2356.640	1.477
Agriculture	15	274.500	274.5	10.607	0.039
Publishing	63	419.500	419.5	44.548	0.106
Assets:					
Finance	86366	17066.300	6237.0	24843.800	1.456
Trading and Commerce	1147	352.571	249.0	333.493	0.046
Contracting	1066	3570.500	189.0	415.761	1.163
Manufacturing	32767	3340.650	1020.0	7451.200	2.230
Public Utilities	24533	13001.300	18121.0	11770.000	0.905
Diversified	19684	1963.500	664.0	4532.530	2.308
Agriculture	439	780.500	780.5	310.420	0.398
Publishing	68	212.000	212.0	48.083	0.227
Employment:					
Finance	6721	1948.380	963.0	2198.150	1.128
Trading and Commerce	3982	977.714	700.0	959.065	0.981
Contracting	8780	3458.330	2815.0	3359.490	0.971
Manufacturing	8646	1301.750	871.5	1902.040	1.461
Public Utilities	23349	6823.570	6411.0	8059.670	1.181
Diversified	19970	3118.950	2000.0	4068.360	1.304
Agriculture	144	1422.000	1422.0	101.823	0.072
Publishing	1527	1246.500	1246.5	1079.750	0.866

Notes:
1. The range of values assumed by the variable under consideration.
2. Median value, designed to reduce the effect of extreme observations on the central tendency measure.
3. Standard deviation.
4. Coefficient of variation as a relative measure of dispersion.

Third, the values of the coefficients of variation suggest that the volume of turnover varies most sharply amongst enterprises engaged in manufacturing while the value of assets varies most severely amongst enterprises engaged in diversified activities. The coefficients of variation suggest the variations in the numbers employed are highest in manufacturing and lowest in agriculture.

Fourth, the high values of coefficients of variation suggest the existence of a high degree of heterogeneity amongst large enterprises in the same (or similar) lines of activity. A detailed study of individual enterprises would reveal that some of these enterprises are not fully utilising their productive capacity while others are overstaffed.

Fifth, the degree of dispersion was most apparent in manufacturing, diversified activities and finance. Only in these lines of activity did the standard deviation tend to exceed the mean value for each variable (that is, turnover, assets and employment).

In order to study the nature of the relationship between volume of turnover, value of assets and the number employed in each line of activity, we estimated the following regressions:

$$Q = a_0 + a_1 N + \Sigma$$

$$Q = ß_0 + ß_1 A + \mu$$

$$Q = \partial_0 + \partial_1 N + \partial_2 A + \pi$$

$$LnQ = y_0 + y_1 LnN + y_2 LnA + v$$

where Q is the volume of turnover; N are the numbers employed; A is the value of assets; and ß, μ, π and v are random variables.

The fourth regression represents a unitary elasticity of substitution function of the Cobb–Douglas type. However, it should be understood that we are not measuring a typical production relationship where output is taken as a function of factor inputs. In most cases we are measuring relationships for firms dealing in heterogeneous products or services. Thus we cannot, strictly speaking, estimate a production function, but only a relationship between the value of turnover on the one hand and the value of assets and numbers employed on the other.[2]

Table 11.2 presents the results for each line of activity except agriculture and publishing and advertising, where the paucity of data did not permit statistical evaluation.

Because of apparent multicollinearity, we could not measure the individual importance of the asset and employment variables on the turnover variable within the multiple regression framework, where insignificant coefficients abound. Hence we based our conclusions on the simple regressions, as follows.

Table 11.2 Regression results

Activity	*Cons.*	*N*	*A*	*LnN*	*LnA*	R^2	F
Finance:							
Q	73.719	0.879	–	–	–	0.664	22.681
	(0.139)	(4.762)					
Q	214.072	–	0.092	–	–	0.940	188.24
	(1.087)		(13.720)				
Q	169.309	0.064	0.087	–	–	0.935	87.459
	(0.747)	(0.457)	(7.099)				
LnQ	1.467	–	–	0.561	0.186	0.774	21.548
	(1.706)			(3.713)	(2.109)		
Trading and commerce:							
Q	372.173	0.076	–	–	–	0.091	3.006
	(6.302)	(1.734)					
Q	319.768	–	0.358	–	–	0.338	11.196
	(6.221)		(3.346)				
Q	329.762	–0.052	0.473	–	–	0.329	5.911
	(6.225)	(–0.874)	(2.783)				
LnQ	4.578	–	–	–0.021	0.286	0.270	4.692
	(7.321)			(–0.276)	(3.014)		
Contracting:							
Q	669.534	–0.013	–	–	–	–0.238	–0.0397
	(2.294)	(–0.199)					
Q	325.790	–	0.840	–	–	0.588	8.137
	(2.122)		(2.852)				
Q	325.083	0.0002	0.840	–	–	0.451	3.051
	(1.355)	(0.0004)	(2.452)				
LnQ	5.358	–	–	0.034	0.135	–0.397	0.289
	(3.094)			(0.175)	(0.739)		
Manufacturing:							
Q	381.636	1.371	–	–	–	0.385	12.871
	(0.441)	(3.588)					
Q	1019.51	–	0.343	–	–	0.368	12.060
	(1.290)		(3.473)				
Q	563.709	0.905	0.127	–	–	0.356	6.252
	(0.579)	(0.817)	(0.450)				
LnQ	1.768	–	–	0.161	0.551	0.481	9.819
	(1.297)			(0.653)	(3.182)		

Table 11.2 *Continued*

Activity	*Cons.*	*N*	*A*	*LnN*	*LnA*	R^2	F
Public utilities:							
Q	–170.986	0.318	–	–	–	0.962	154.70
	(–0.662)	(12.438)					
Q	730.462	–	0.098	–	–	0.033	1.206
	(0.485)		(1.098)				
Q	15.023	0.366	–0.024	–	–	0.966	85.724
	(0.052)	(11.719)	(–1.222)				
LnQ	1.853	–	–	0.409	0.220	0.676	7.264
	(0.988)			(1.105)	(1.075)		
Diversified:							
Q	929.538	0.214	–	–	–	0.093	3.148
	(1.528)	(1.774)					
Q	743.610	–	0.434	–	–	0.682	45.969
	(2.398)		(6.780)				
Q	586.951	0.062	0.416	–	–	0.676	22.916
	(1.596)	(0.810)	(6.804)				
LnQ	2.359	–	–	0.038	0.640	0.707	26.288
	(3.107)	–	–	(0.321)	(5.693)		

Notes: The figures in brackets refer to the estimated *t*-statistics for each of the estimated regression coefficients; R^2 is the adjusted coefficient of determination; *F* is the value of *F* statistics.

First, there is a significant positive relationship between turnover value and number employed in all major enterprises with the exception of contracting, where enterprises with the highest turnover values are not necessarily those with highest employment.

Second, there is a significant and strong positive relationship between volume of turnover and value of assets in all major business enterprises with the exception of those engaged in public utilities.

Third, the logarithmic regression testing the relationship between turnover and assets and employment suggest that:

1. The elasticity of turnover with respect to employment is insignificant and quite low in all activities but finance. This result may be due to the above-mentioned multicollinearity problem.

2. The volume of turnover has a significant and inelastic response with respect to the value of assets in the various business enterprises, except those engaged in contracting and public utilities.
3. The turnover of enterprises engaged in finance would seem to be subject to decreasing returns to scale with respect to assets and employment where the value of $Y_1 + Y_2$ is less than one in this line of activity.
4. There is no significant relationship between turnover value and number employed in enterprises engaged in diversified activities. This is expected given the high degree of heterogeneity in these industries.[3]

PERFORMANCE RATIOS ANALYSIS

In order to assess the economic performance of the sample enterprises, for each one we calculated:

1. Value of turnover per employee (*Q*/*N*)
2. Value of turnover per *SR* of assets (*Q*/*A*)
3. The assets–labour ratio (*A*/*N*)

The first coefficient (*Q*/*N*) represents an index of average labour productivity, while the second (*Q*/*A*) represents an index of capital productivity. The assets–labour ratio coefficient (*A*/*N*) is a proxy for the degree of capital intensity.

Table 11.3 gives the above coefficients for each enterprise in each line of activity. The table also gives, for each coefficient, the usual summary statistics of the range, the mean, the median, the standard deviation and the coefficient of variation.

The statistical results of Table 11.3 suggest the following.

First, business enterprises engaged in manufacturing have the highest mean turnover per employee, while those engaged in agriculture and public utilities have the lowest mean turnover per employee.

Second, agriculture and the financial institutions have the lowest mean turnover per asset while enterprises engaged in contracting and trading and commerce have the highest mean turnover per asset.

Table 11.3 Some basic indicators of performance

Enterprise	*Q/N*	*Q/A*	*A/N*
Finance:			
National Commercial Bank	1.295	0.103	12.591
Riyadh Bank	0.840	0.081	10.354
Saudi American Bank	2.408	0.082	29.315
Al Rajhi Banking and Investment Corporation	0.306	0.090	3.395
Saudi French Bank	1.187	5.996	0.198
Arabi National Bank	0.520	0.091	5.730
Saudi British Bank	1.216	0.080	15.138
Saudi Cairo Bank	0.808	0.615	1.314
United Saudi Commercial Bank	1.908	0.080	23.897
Saudi Hollandi Bank	0.444	0.771	0.576
Al Jazira Bank	0.605	1.282	0.472
Saudi Investment Bank	1.276	0.069	18.404
National Insurance Company	2.000	0.614	3.258
Range	2.103	5.927	29.117
Mean	1.139	0.766	9.588
Median	1.187	0.091	5.730
Standard deviation	0.648	1.617	9.688
Coefficient of variation	0.569	2.112	1.010
Trading and commerce:			
Al Jeraisy Group	0.303	0.758	0.400
Al Hamrani and Al Salman	0.994	0.941	1.056
Al Bahrawi Trading Company	1.190	5.992	0.199
Jamjoom Trading Establishment	0.302	1.809	0.168
Al Ajou Establishment	0.780	1.950	0.400
Al Eisa and Sons	1.222	1.833	0.667
Alpha Trading and Shipping	27.778	1.000	27.778
Suliman Al Rajhi and Sons	0.119	0.398	0.298
Rolaco Trading and Contracting	2.163	1.957	1.106
Farouq and Mamoun Tamr and Company	0.796	1.530	0.520
Al Goureshi and Company	0.678	2.288	0.296
Siddieg and Mohamed Attar Company	0.609	4.972	0.122
Amic	0.500	2.059	0.243
Al Arjan and Company	0.496	1.394	0.256
Al Rajab and A. Sisila and Company	0.399	0.791	0.504
Al Gouseibi General Trading	0.569	1.800	0.316
Abbar Company	0.563	4.500	0.125
Al Bararji Company	0.623	4.698	0.133
Gabani and Company	0.224	1.587	0.141
Al Dries Company	0.223	0.573	0.389
Al Tayar Group	0.232	1.487	0.156
Range	27.659	5.593	27.655
Mean	1.941	2.110	1.684
Median	0.569	1.800	0.316

Table 11.3 *Continued*

Enterprise	*Q/N*	*Q/A*	*A/N*
Standard deviation	5.938	1.565	5.989
Coefficient of variation	3.059	0.742	3.553
Contracting and maintenance:			
Al Mabani Group	0.421	1.353	0.311
Al Baydaa Company	0.307	41.250	0.007
Al Aswad Company Limited	2.323	0.826	2.814
Samama Company	0.044	2.667	0.017
Sarbas Roads and Maintenance Company	0.938	7.500	0.125
Saudi Services and Operations Company	0.063	1.518	0.041
Range	2.278	40.425	2.806
Mean	0.683	9.185	0.553
Median	0.364	2.092	0.083
Standard deviation	0.867	15.897	1.113
Coefficient of variation	1.270	1.731	2.015
Manufacturing:			
Saudi Arabian Mobil	3.941	1.678	2.348
Petromin-Mobil Limited	10.376	1.771	5.858
Saudi Basic Lidustries Company (SABIC)	1.053	0.279	3.776
Saudi Petrochemicals	2.829	0.237	11.921
Al Rajhi Industrial and Commercial Company	1.518	8.315	0.183
Saudi Cables	0.651	0.950	0.685
Riyadh Cables	1.656	2.366	0.700
Saudi Vegetable Oil and Ghee (SAVOLA)	0.722	1.333	0.579
Salb	2.083	2.778	0.750
Petromin Lubricating Oils	8.759	0.845	10.370
National Methanol	1.817	0.303	5.991
Southern Province Cement Company	0.436	0.324	1.348
Gas and Manufacturing National Company	0.255	0.320	0.795
Saudi Fruit Juice and Beverage industries	2.000	3.529	0.567
Arabian Cement Company	0..574	0.290	1.980
Yamama Cement Company	0.260	0.221	1.177
Saudi Bahraini Cement Company	0.275	0.233	1.183
Saudi Cement Company	0.261	0.355	0.715
Saudi Fisheries Company	0.213	1.242	0.171
Halawani Brothers	0.232	1.487	0.156
Range	10.163	8.094	11.765
Mean	1.998	1.443	2.564
Median	0.912	0.898	0.986
Standard deviation	2.789	1.880	3.404
Coefficient of variation	1.396	1.303	1.328

Table 11.3 *Continued*

Enterprise	*Q/N*	*Q/A*	*A/N*
Public utilities:			
Saudi Arabian Airlines Company	0.322	0.424	0.760
SCECO East	0.320	0.085	3.780
SCECO West	0.219	0.068	3.250
SCECO Central	0.220	0.065	3.366
Saudi Arabian National Shipping	1.169	0.481	2.431
STTB	0.485	7.121	0.068
SAPTCO	0.102	0.531	0.192
Range	1.067	7.056	3.712
Mean	0.405	1.253	1.978
Median	0.320	0.424	2.431
Standard deviation	0.357	2.596	1.598
Coefficient of variation	0.881	2.071	0.808
Diversified:			
Abdul Latif Jamael Company	2.207	0.938	2.353
Sallat Al Baraka Group	0.946	0.344	2.752
Zenel Industries Limited	0.139	1.188	0.124
Al Faddl Group	0.764	8.456	0.090
Al Rashid Investment Group	0.886	2.477	0.358
Abdula Alireza	0.861	1.539	0.559
Al Faisalia Group	0.603	1.455	0.414
Al Olyan Saudi Holding Company (OSHCO)	0.598	1.098	0.544
Al Qahtani and Sons	0.620	2.443	0.254
Trading and Industrial Group Limited	0.444	1.333	0.333
Al Khorief Sons Group	0.455	0.882	0.515
Al Tamimi Group	0.206	0.600	0.343
Saudi Establishment for Catering and Commerce	0.214	0.913	0.234
Al Hamrani Group	0.314	0.923	0.340
Al Agad and Company	0.161	0.869	0.185
Saudi Investment and Marketing Company	15.367	1.760	8.733
Al Amoundi Saudi Group	0.168	1.668	0.101
Abu Nayan and Sons	0.250	1.094	0.229
Alamdar Trading and Contracting Limited	0.778	2.273	0.342
Al Hoshan	0.163	1.121	0.145
Saudi Baili Heavy Industries	0.148	1.067	0.139
Al Zahri Group for Trading and Contracting	0.484	4.136	0.117
Range	15.228	8.112	8.643
Mean	1.217	1.750	0.873
Median	0.469	1.119	0.336
Standard deviation	3.193	1.708	1.884
Coefficient of variation	1.624	0.976	2.158

Table 11.3 *Continued*

Enterprise	*Q/N*	*Q/A*	*A/N*
Agriculture:			
Hail Agriculture Development Company	0.209	0.503	0.416
NADEC	0.179	0.267	0.669
Range	0.030	0.236	0.254
Mean	0.194	0.385	0.542
Median	0.194	0.385	0.542
Standard deviation	0.021	0.167	0.179
Coefficient of variation	0.110	0.443	0.331
Publishing:			
Saudi International Research and Marketing	0.224	1.833	0.122
Tihama Advertising, Public Relations and Marketing	0.803	2.180	0.369
Range	0.579	0.346	0.246
Mean	0.514	2.007	0.245
Median	0.514	2.007	0.245
Standard deviation	0.409	0.245	0.174
Coefficient of variation	0.797	0.122	0.709

Third, the highest mean asset–labour ratio exists in enterprises engaged in finance, while the lowest asset–labour ratio exists in enterprises engaged in publishing and advertisement, agriculture and contracting. This may be explained by the fact that bank assets include deposit accounts and by the fact that agriculture and the contracting industry are move dependent on labour for their activities.

Fourth, the picture remains largely the same for the turnover–asset and asset–labour ratios if the median measure of central tendency is used instead of the mean.

Fifth, most of the enterprises seem to be using different capital–labour ratios. Thus two firms with similar turnover per employee could be using quite different asset–employment ratios. This may be explained to a great extent by the high degree of heterogeneity between firms and the existence of excess capacity.

Sixth, the value of turnover per employee and the value of assets per employee are much closer in enterprises engaged in agriculture and finance than in other enterprises. This may be explained by the smallness of the sample and the choice of optimum sizes and scales in the case of agriculture and by the relatively higher degree of competition that exists between the banks. Turnover per asset has the lowest variation for publishing, agriculture, and trading and commerce.

Seventh, the productivity of labour varies mostly among enterprises engaged in trading and commerce, while the productivity of assets varies mostly among enterprises engaged in finance and utilities. The asset–labour ratio varies mostly among firms engaged in diversified activities.

Finally, a detailed comparison of average productivity that is, turnover per employee and turnover per asset, suggests the existence of excess capacity in a number of the business enterprises. It also suggests that some enterprises are overstaffed. Firms engaged in the production of cement and electricity are clear examples of capacity excess.

We also tested to see whether there is any relationship between the productivity of labour – as measured by the value of turnover per employee, a proxy for the productivity of capital as measured by the value of turnover per SR of assets – and the capital–labour ratio or capital intensity, as measured by the value of assets per employee. These tests were carried out by using simple linear and log-linear regressions as follows:

$$(Q/N) = \partial_0 + \partial_1 (Q/N) + u$$

$$(Q/A) = \surd_0 + \surd_1 (A/N) + v$$

$$Ln(Q/N) = k_0 + k_1 Ln(A/N) + w$$

$$Ln(Q/A) = \emptyset_0 + \emptyset_1 Ln(A/N) + e$$

where Q, A and N are as defined before and u, v, w and e are the regression errors. The regression results are given in Table 11.4.

From these results it is possible to derive the following conclusions. First, there is a strong positive relationship between labour productivity and capital intensity in all enterprises except those engaged in public utilities. This is confirmed for both

Table 11.4 Regression results

Activity	*Cons.*	*A/N*	*Ln(A/N)*	R^2	*F*
Finance:					
Q/N	0.685	0.047	–	0.458	11.129
	(3.602)	(3.336)			
Q/A	1.452	–0.0723	–	0.110	2.479
	(2.390)	(–1.575)			
Ln (Q/N)	–0.295	–	0.182	0.159	3.266
	(–1.377)		(1.807)		
Ln (Q/A)	–0.295	–	0.818	0.844	65.929
	(–1.377)		(–8.120)		
Trading and Commerce:					
Q/N	0.273	0.991	–	0.997	59.057
	(3.480)	(76.849)			
Q/A	2.190	–0.047	–	–0.018	0.643
	(6.106)	(–0.802)			
Ln (Q/N)	0.270	–	0.755	0.636	35.909
	(1.417)		(5.992)		
Ln (Q/A)	0.270	–	–0.214	0.122	3.786
	(1.417)		(–1.946)		
Contracting:					
Q/N	0.279	0.730	–	0.850	29.296
	(1.789)	(5.413)			
Q/A	11.535	–4.251	–	–0.139	0.389
	(1.463)	(–0.624)			
Ln (Q/N)	0.074	–	0.527	0.439	4.911
	(0.100)		(2.216)		
Ln (Q/A)	0.074	–	–0.473	0.370	3.942
	(0.1000)		(–1.985)		
Manufacturing:					
Q/N	0.660	0.522	–	0.373	12.278
	(1.058)	(3.504)			
Q/A	1.839	–0.155	–	0.027	1.529
	(3.510)	(–1.237)			
Ln (Q/N)	–0.139	–	0.587	0.347	11.096
	(–0.628)		(3.331)		
Ln (Q/A)	–0.139	–	–0.413	0.192	5.507
	(–0.628)		(–2.347)		
Public Utilities:					
Q/N	0.381	0.012	–	–0.196	0.016
	(1.545)	(0.125)			
Q/A	3.128	–0.948	–	0.209	2.581
	(2.147)	(–1.607)			

Table 11.4 *Continued*

Activity	*Cons.*	*A/N*	*Ln(A/N)*	R^2	*F*
Ln (Q/N)	–1.165	–	0.066	–0.176	0.101
	(–3.753)		(0.318)		
Ln (Q/A)	–1.165	–	–0.934	0.760	19.954
	(–3.753)		(–4.467)		
Diversified:					
Q/N	–0.204	1.628	–	0.918	236.65
	(–0.945)	(15.383)			
Q/A	1.830	–0.092	–	–0.039	1.741
	(4.456)	(–0.455)			
Ln (Q/N)	0.080	–	0.782	0.657	41.185
	(0.432)		(6.418)		
Ln (Q/A)	0.080	–	–0.218	0.095	3.193
	(0.432)		(–1.787)		

linear and logarithmic models. Firms with the largest assets per employee in this last line of activity do not necessarily have the highest turnover per employee. This may suggest the existence of 'excess capacity'.[4]

Second, the linear model indicates no significant relationship between the productivity of capital and the degree of capital intensity in all enterprises. On closer examination this might suggest a failing of the model itself and hence inferences should be drawn from the alternative logarithmic form, where a number of significant relationships are detectable. Specifically, there is a significant negative relationship between productivity of capital and asset–employment ratios among enterprises engaged in finance, manufacturing and utilities. Somewhat surprisingly, enterprises with higher asset–employment ratios turned out to have lower turnover–asset ratios. This may suggest that capital is not optimally utilised in these enterprises.

CONCLUSIONS

This chapter has attempted to analyse data on Saudi business enterprises. Despite the data limitations it was possible to reach some important conclusions, which can be summarised as follows:

1. There is a significant, strong, positive relationship between turnover value, number employed and value of assets in most of the enterprises.
2. The elasticity of turnover with respect to employment is quite low in all enterprises but those engaged in finance.
3. The turnover of all enterprises seems to be subject to decreasing returns to scale with respect to employment and assets.
4. The productivity of labour varies most among enterprises engaged in trading and commerce, while the productivity of assets varies most among those in finance and utilities. Also, the asset–labour ratio varies most among firms with diversified activities.
5. There is a strong positive relationship between labour productivity and capital intensity in all major enterprises except those engaged in utilities.
6. There is no relationship between the productivity of capital and the degree of capital intensity in all the major enterprises in the sample.
7. There is a significant negative relationship between the productivity of capital and the degree of capital intensity in enterprises engaged in finance, manufacturing and utilities.
8. Some enterprises are overstaffed.
9. There is some evidence of excess capacity in some business enterprises.
10. Capital does not seem to be optimally utilised in some business enterprises.

References

1. *Arab News*, vol. 22, no. 223 (1986), pp. 14–17.
2. D. F. Heathfield, *Production Functions* (London: Macmillan, 1971) p. 15.
3. W.T. Baumol, *Business Behavior, Value and Growth* (New York: Macmillan, 1959), p. 122.
4. J. Dean, *Managerial Economics* (Englewood Cliffs, NJ: Prentice Hall, 1951), p. 234.

12 The Role of the Controller in the Saudi Basic Industries Corporation

Sulayman H. Atieh[1]

This chapter presents the findings of an empirical study that investigated the role of the controller in the Al-Jubail area affiliates of the Saudi Basic Industries Corporation (SABIC), located in the Al-Jubail area. SABIC, a Saudi joint stock company with capital of SR 10 billion, was incorporated in 1976 under Royal Decree number M/66. Its purpose has been to establish large-scale, capital-intensive foundry industries that utilise the Kingdom's hydrocarbon resources, particularly natural gas and natural liquid gas, and to provide intermediate industrial products for the secondary industries in the private sector. When completed, the capital investments of SABIC will have reached SR 54 billion. SABIC operates primarily through joint venture partnerships with a number of leading multinational industrial corporations, such as the Mitsubishi Gas Company, Celanese Corporation, Texas Eastern Corporation, Exxon Chemical Company, Shell Oil Company, Taiwan Fertilizer Company and others.[2]

The controller is the organisation's chief financial officer, who is responsible for overall financial and management accounting functions in relation to the firms' management decision-making, analysis, planning, implementation and control activities. Garrison[3] states that even though the controllers do not have line authority, they are in a special position to exercise authority through reporting and interpreting the data needed in decision making. Tipgos, Holmes and Lander[4] concluded that the role of the controller in helping top management to make strategic decisions is quite extensive; 68 per cent of the respondents (the president and executive vice presidents of Fortune 500 companies) reported that they relied heavily on the controller for advice when making strategic decisions. Most importantly, 37 per cent of the respondents indicated that they could not make strategic decisions without consulting the controller. Boyd and Fleming[5] stated that more progressive firms have redefined the controller's duties to include planning, interpreting, evaluating, consulting and appraising economic activities. They note the role of the computer in revolutionising the controller's position from a generator of data to an interpreter of information.

Williams[6] conducted a study on the role of the controller in the Minnesota Mining and Manufacturing Company (3M). He reported that the controller described his role as providing 'an independent and objective assessment of the financial performance of 3M's various organizations.' He added, 'Our controllers view their role as not to always challenge management, but as being cooperative in an effort to develop a better business.' The study revealed that 3M controllers are involved in budgeting, forecasting and analysis for new equipment and capital expenditures, and the development of new products, as well as preparing financial statements and allocating costs to operating units. In addition Williams' study established that division controllers in 3M are viewed as business advisors and financial consultants who are part of the operating/decision-making team. With these variations of the controllers' duties, the author considered 3M as a model for management accounting excellence.

Sathe[7] conducted an empirical study on the role of the controller's function in large (sales of $300 million or more) multidivisional US corporations. The study emphasised the controller's involvement in managerial functions. This role required a broad insight into various functions of management and a detailed knowledge of accounting and financial analysis. Boyd and Flemming[8] reported that present-day controllers need to be familiar with concepts from humanities, management, computer science, economics and general business practices in order to be able to exercise their broadened responsibilities. Frishkoff[9] indicates that the controller is an integral and vital part of the management team. Moreover the controller must have personal integrity and be trusted by all employees and the public. Horngren and Sundem[10] stated that in

General Electric the controller is a key executive who aids managerial planning and control in over 160 company subdivisions. The controller maintains authority by reporting and interpreting relevant data, and exerts a force or influence on decision- making, or projects attitudes that impel management towards logical decisions that are consistent with objectives.

The purpose of the study described in this chapter was to investigate controllers' of the Saudi Basic Industries Corporation and to determine their involvement in providing managers with information for planning, controlling and decision making. It examined the organisational status of the controller, the organisational structure of the controller's department, and the personal characteristics and qualifications of the controllers. The findings of the study will be used as guidelines for:

1. Identifying changes in controllers' functions and the expansion of their role in the organisation.
2. Determining the degree of controller involvement in managerial functions.
3. Examining the difficulties facing the controller in meeting managers' information requirements.
4. Discovering characteristics associated with the development of strong controllers.

The financial executives of firms established by SABIC were asked to respond to a questionnaire survey. The questionnaire was written in English for the benefit of foreign financial executives working in SABIC (the questionnaire is available to the reader upon request). The questionnaire was divided into the following five sections:

1. *Organisational status of the controller*. This section included questions on the position of the controller's department in the organisational chart, the role of the controller in the management team, and the importance and prestige of the controller within the organisation.
2. *Organisational structure of the controller's department*. This section included questions on how the controller's office is organised and an open-ended question on the controller's

administrative responsibility for electronic data processing operations.

3. *Functions of the controller.* The financial executives were asked to assess the degree of involvement of the controller in managerial functions. Degree of involvement was divided into five categories, ranging from 'no involvement' to 'very strong involvement.' The managerial functions[11] included in this study are shown in Table 12.1.
4. *Characteristics of the information provided by the controller.* This section included questions on the relevancy and sufficiency of the information prepared by the controller and its value to managerial decisions. The section also included an open-ended question on the major difficulties that might face the controller in supplying managers with their information requirements.
5. *Characteristics of strong controllers.* The financial executives were asked to rate characteristics of strong controllers with regard to their importance. The importance of these characteristics were explored on a four-point scale ranging from 'not important' to 'very important.' Characteristics included are shown in Table 12.2. Some of these characteristics are taken from Sathe,[12] who enumerated the characteristics of strong controllers without attempting to rank them according to their importance.

The SABIC affiliates that participated in this study were Saudi European Petrochemical Co., Saudi Iron & Steel Co., Al-Jubail Fertilizer Co., Arabian Petrochemical Co., National Plastic Co., National Industrial Gases Co., Eastern Petrochemical Co., Saudi Petrochemical Co., National Methanol Co. and Saudi Methanol Co.

The questionnaires were delivered to financial executives from the ten companies involved in the survey. Respondents included financial managers, cost control and budgeting managers, and vice-presidents for finance and administration. All the findings reported in this chapter are based on the responses of those executives. The sample size was representative as the respondents represented 10 of the 12 SABIC companies in the Al-Jubail area.

Table 12.1 Degree of involvement of the controllers in SABIC affiliates in managerial functions (per cent)

Functions of the controller	*No involvement*	*Low involvement*	*Average involvement*	*Strong involvement*	*Very strong involvement*
1. Preparing and interpreting the financial statements and reports of the company	–	8	16	25	51
2. Participating in forecasting sales, net income, capital expenditures and cash flow	–	–	34	50	16
3. Preparing in conjunction with other officers and department heads an annual budget, covering all activities of the company, for submission to top management prior to the beginning of fiscal year	–	–	–	42	58
4. Accumulating and analysing actual costs	–	8	25	42	25
5. Preparing and analysing performance reports (comparison of actual budget data)	–	–	16	34	50
6. Consulting with management as to the meaning of cost information	–	–	–	42	58
7. Participating in the control of cost through the means of reports analysing the causes of variances between actual and standard costs	–	–	25	33	42
8. Providing information for special decisions (such as the removal or addition of a product line and manufacture or purchase of component parts)	–	–	35	33	42

Table 12.1 *Continued*

Functions of the controller	*No involvement*	*Low involvement*	*Average involvement*	*Strong involvement*	*Very strong involvement*
9. Designing, installing and maintaining computer-based information systems	–	16	25	59	–
10. Preparing, analysing and interpreting financial results for utilisation by management in the decision-making process	–	–	8	59	33
11. Preparing and filing external reports as required to satisfy government regulatory bodies, stockholders and financial institution	–	8	34	25	33
12. Providing advice to management on the financial implications of decisions under consideration	–	–	–	34	66

Table 12.2 Characteristics of strong controllers rated according to their importance

Characteristics of a strong controller	*Average ratings*	*Ranking*
1. Personal integrity and professional commitment	2.75	1
2. Ability to judge what is important to management and to make recommendations	2.66	2
3. Personal energy and motivation	2.58	3
4. Demonstrations of a high degree of initiative	2.58	3
5. Understanding of what management needs to run the business effectively	2.50	5
6. Ability to translate the facts and statistics into trends and relationships	2.42	6
7. Accuracy in findings and reporting	2.42	6
8. Ability to develop and provide information as quickly as possible	2.42	6
9. Accounting knowledge	2.42	6
10. Ability to express ideas clearly in writing or in making information presentations	2.42	6
11. Understanding of the company, including its technologies, products, policies, objectives, organisation and environment	2.33	11
12. Knowledge of planning	2.33	11
13. Analytical skill	2.50	13
14. Ability to gain the confidence of other executives by providing accurate and timely information with an attitude of wanting to help that is not perceived as threatening	2.20	14
15. Ability to build relationships and develop influence	1.83	15

ANALYSIS OF THE RESULTS

Organisational Status of the Controller

One important finding is that the controller in SABIC industries is an important and integral part of the management team. Fifty per cent of the respondents indicated that the position of the controller's department is at the top of the organisational chart; 57 per cent stated that the controller is an executive officer at the policy-making level; 75 per cent said that the controller reports directly to the president of the company or to the board of directors; and 95 per cent considered that the controller is an integral part of the management team.

Organisational Structure of the Controller's Department

The study revealed that approximately 75 per cent of respondents reported having organisational charts for the controller's department. The main functions of this department were given as general accounting, cost accounting, and financial planning and control. Moreover 75 per cent of the sample reported that internal auditors are independent and do not report to the controller; they report either to the finance and administrative general manager or directly to the president of the company. Eighty-five per cent of the respondents indicated that controllers do not have direct administrative responsibility for electronic data processing (EDP) operations. These respondents gave the following reasons:

1. EDP involves non-financial operations.
2. As it serves the whole company, EDP should have total responsibility of automation and systems integration.
3. Many jobs are accomplished by EDP that the controller has no access to.
4. EDP serves many departments, such as production, maintenance and materials.

Functions of the Controller

Traditionally the controller is concerned with financial functions. However the study revealed that the functions of the controllers in SABIC industries are not restricted to financial matters. Table 13.1 shows that the controllers of SABIC companies are strongly involved in a number of managerial functions. All respondents indicated the controllers are strongly in preparing annual budgets and providing advice to management on the meaning of cost information and the financial implications of decisions under consideration. In addition, 84 per cent reported that the controllers are heavily involved in preparing and analysing performance reports, and 75 per cent said that the controllers are heavily involved in providing information for special decisions.

The respondents provided strong evidence that controllers in SABIC industries play an important role in cost saving. The policics and procedures followed to achieve this function were summarised by the respondents as follows:

1. Combining the functions of two or more departments into one department.
2. Hiring qualified personnel for the controller's department to help increase productivity.
3. Analysing project costs to discover inefficiencies in material, machinery and manpower.
4. Reviewing with department heads any deviations of actual against planned expenditures to provide the manager with appropriate advice to implement corrective actions.

Characteristics of the Information Provided by the Controller

Another important finding of this study is that the controllers in SABIC industries are able to provide department managers with valuable information. Eighty-five per cent of respondents believe that management decisions have improved as a result of the information submitted by controllers. Nevertheless the respondents indicated that the controllers face difficulties in meeting managers' information requirements. The respondents cited the following difficulties:

1. Managers lack knowledge of financial accounting, finance, budgeting and cost control techniques.
2. Defining the real information needs of the managers.
3. The substantial effort and time that is necessary for designing a computer system to collect information and present it in different reporting formats.

Characteristics and Qualifications of Strong Controllers

The characteristics of strong controllers, shown in Table 13.2, were rated according to a four-point scale, ranging from 'not important' (0) to very 'important' (3). These ratings were converted in to average ratings, as reflected in Table 13.2, which also points out that competent controllers should not only have a broad knowledge of accounting, but should also possess a number of other characteristics, including personal integrity, professional commitment and the ability to judge what is important to management and to make recommendations.

CONCLUSIONS

The study reveals that the controllers in SABIC affiliates are strongly involved in managerial functions, such as participating in the preparation of annual, preparing and analysing performance reports, and providing advice to management on the financial implications of decisions under consideration. Moreover controllers play a vital role in the control and rationalisation of costs. This function is implemented by drawing managerial attention to inefficiencies and by reporting the causes of discrepancies between actual and budgeted costs. The study also identified the most important characteristics of strong controllers. These are personal integrity and the ability to judge what is important to management, demonstrate a high degree of initiative, translate facts into trends and relationships, and gain the confidence of executives by providing accurate and timely information and accounting knowledge.

Notes and References

1. The author would like to express his appreciation to Dr Secil Tuncalp, Professor of Marketing, and Dr Mohamed Ali Mirghani, Chairman of Department of Accounting and Management Information Systems at King Fahd University of Petroleum & Minerals, for their valuable comments and suggestions. The author would also like to thank Abdulwahhab Al-Rahman Dahlawi for his assistance in distributing and collecting the questionnaires.
2. *Adding to Value of the Kingdom's Natural Resources* (Riyadh: SABIC, 1986), p. 9.
3. R. Garrison, *Managerial Accounting Concepts for Planning, Control, Decision Making* (Texas: Business Publications, 1988), p. 10.
4. M. Tipgos, J. Holmes and G. Lander, 'The Management Accountant Today: A Status Report', *Management Accounting*, November 1983, pp. 53–7.

5. P. Boyd and M. Flemming, 'Productivity: The Controller's Role', *Management Accounting*, September 1987, pp. 28–32.
6. K. Williams, 'The Magic of 3M Management Accounting Excellence', *Management Accounting*, November 1983, pp. 53–7.
7. V. Sathe, *Controller Involvement in Management* (New Jersey: Prentice Hall, 1982), p. 100.
8. P. Boyd and M. Flemming, 'Productivity: The Controller's Role', *Management Accounting*, September 1987, pp. 28–32.
9. P. A. Frishkoff, 'Is Your Controllership Function Out of Control?', *Management Accounting*, March 1986, pp. 45–85.
10. Charles T. Horngren and Gary L. Sundem, *Introduction to Management Accounting*, 8th edn (New York: National Association of Accountants, 1982), pp. 12–13.
11. W. Morse and H. Roth, *Cost Accounting Processing, Evaluating and Using Cost Data*, 3rd edn (New York: National Association of Accountants, 1982), p. 8.
12. V. Sathe, *Controller Involvement in Management*, (New Jersey: Prentice Hall, 1982), pp. 141–3.

Epilogue

Business and Economic Development in Saudi Arabia has provided a forum for its contributors to provide an insight into the cultural, economic, legal and social values that have shaped the commercial sector development planning efforts in Saudi Arabia. The Kingdom is too often perceived as a desert country without real industry, or it is perceived as being so wealthy from oil revenues that it need not worry about developing real industry. Neither of these perceptions is true. Upon closer examination the Kingdom exhibits diversity and vitality, based on an Islamic and Arabian heritage that it is both confining and yielding to the business development process. The influence of rapid, oil-financed modernisation has obviously added new dimensions to the Saudi Arabian economy that are unlike any other in the world, but rather than purchase Western lifestyles wholesale, Saudi planners have chosen to create a pattern of development that reflects their community's specific needs. This has allowed the Kingdom to gain political leverage around the globe and at the same time remain focused on raising the standard of living of its people.

With this book we have tried to allay misconceptions about how Saudi Arabia has approached business development. Too many people believe, for example, that the Kingdom has been able to spend unlimited amounts of money only since the 1973 oil embargo. Or they see Saudi government investments as spendthrift purchases of American and European architectural designs and construction. In fact, while much money may have been extracted from many Saudis through inflated corporate price tags, the Saudi government has usually taken a long-term view of commercial sector development. The vast amounts of money spent on construction went mainly to infrastructure projects that allowed businesses to set up manufacturing concerns. Moreover it is interesting for most lay readers to see how the problems faced by Saudi planners are so completely different from those faced by city and state planners in the Americas or Europe.

Our goal in contributing to this collection was to promote a greater understanding of a nation that has been long shrouded in prejudice. The Kingdom of Saudi Arabia has always been a land of great diversity, ranging from the bedouin shepherd family in the desert to the city dwellers in large metropolitan areas. But now it is also home to the most modern facilities and the most ancient traditions in the world. The presence of a strong religious tradition and a rich cultural heritage are enduring in the ever-changing, modernising socioeconomic structure. At the same time, centuries-old principles and values have not been sacrificed in the wake of massive infrastructure construction. These facts make Saudi Arabia a fascinating case study for business, economic and urban development planners. We hope you have enjoyed reading our book, and that it helps you develop business in Saudi Arabia

J. W. WRIGHT, JR

Index

Note: 'n.' after a page reference indicates the number of a note on that page.